The EVERYTHING KIDS'

Snakes, Lizards,

and Other Scaly Creatures Book

Creepy, crawly, slithery fun!

Greg Kroening

⬥ adamsmedia
Avon, Massachusetts

PUBLISHER Karen Cooper
MANAGING EDITOR, EVERYTHING® SERIES Lisa Laing
COPY CHIEF Casey Ebert
ASSISTANT PRODUCTION EDITOR Jo-Anne Duhamel
ACQUISITIONS EDITOR Lisa Laing
DEVELOPMENT EDITOR Lisa Laing
EVERYTHING® SERIES COVER DESIGNER Erin Alexander

An Everything® Series Book.
Everything® and everything.com® are registered trademarks of F+W Media, Inc.

Published by
Adams Media, a division of F+W Media, Inc.
57 Littlefield Street, Avon, MA 02322. U.S.A.
www.adamsmedia.com

ISBN 10: 1-5072-0120-6
ISBN 13: 978-1-5072-0120-6

Printed by LSC Communications, Harrisonburg, VA, U.S.A.

November 2016

10 9 8 7 6 5 4 3 2 1

Many of the designations used by manufacturers and sellers to distinguish their products are claimed as trademarks. Where those designations appear in this book and F+W Media, Inc. was aware of a trademark claim, the designations have been printed with initial capital letters.

Cover design by Erin Alexander.
Cover illustrations by Dana Regan.
Interior illustrations by Kurt Dolber.
Additional interior illustrations © 123RF/Pavel Konovalov, Svetlana Alyuk, Robert Eastman, T Cundrawan, vectorshowstudio.
Puzzles by Scot Ritchie.

This book is available at quantity discounts for bulk purchases.
For information, please call 1-800-289-0963.

Visit the entire Everything® series at www.everything.com.

This book is dedicated to Sam and Owen.
Their excitement and love for all creatures and critters is very cool.

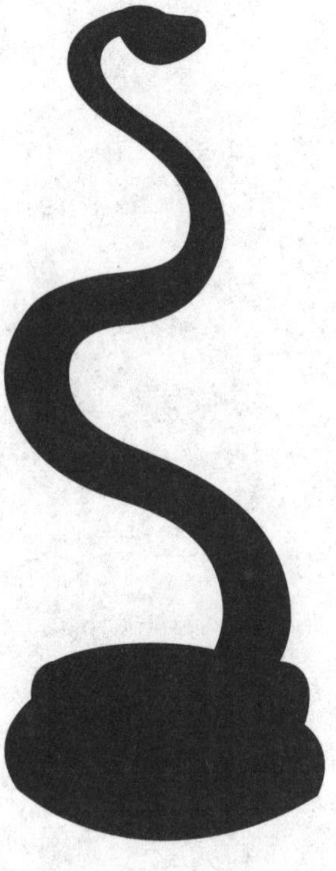

Letter to
Parents and Teachers

We've all heard the old nursery rhyme that said what boys and girls were made of—you know, "blah blah snails, puppy dog tails, and blah blah spice, everything nice." The truth is that boys and girls are really both made of deep knowledge and rich experience. Hands-on, minds-on, and hearts-on study of biology provides that. In this book, the branch of biology that children will learn about is herpetology. This book was written by a teacher and parent of young children who understands that biology by the book and biology outdoors are just as important as reading, writing, and arithmetic (what poor spellers call "the three Rs"). Richard Louv, the author of the bestselling book *Last Child in the Woods*, told adults that our children need more understanding of nature than of pop culture in order to grow up well-rounded and healthy. If this book caught your eye, you probably agree.

This basic focused study in the class of reptiles teaches kids concepts that are key to all biology: naming, classifying, habitat, adaptation, anatomy, and others. First off, children's ability to simply identify and name a scaly creature is really very powerful. Once they learn the name of a creature, they are surprised by how often they see it in media, the zoo, or in the wild. Next, when our kids learned that a square is a kind of rectangle, they learned to do classification. With this book, children learn how biologists similarly put species into groups and those groups into bigger groups. Third, surviving changes in the environment requires reptiles and all living creatures to adapt. Reptiles have developed some of nature's coolest adaptations. Your young reader will enjoy learning about them. When children learn the anatomy of reptiles they can begin to make comparisons and learn how they themselves are built.

Throughout this book as your young reader learns about the world of reptiles, she will be encouraged to put down the book and explore her corner of the world. That requires a few words on respect and safety. Readers young and old, please leave your woods, swamp, or desert the way you found it. Please, do not collect wild species. More on safety will come later in the book.

If your young reader wants a reptile pet, the place to go is a good pet store. This book ends with information on how to buy and care for a healthy reptile. Pet ownership is a great way for children to learn responsibility and sensitivity. The last chapters give practical advice on doing it right. Parents, the ownership decision is up to you. Whatever you decide, enjoy the adventure of nature!

—Greg Kroening

Contents

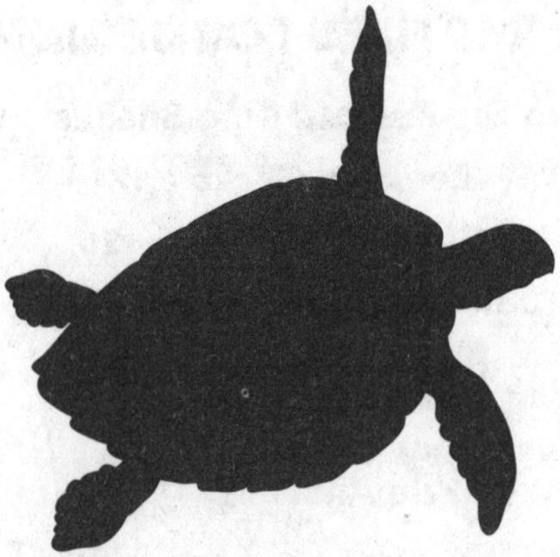

Introduction

Some crawl, some slither, some hiss, most hunt, but they all hide! Who are they? They are the snakes, the lizards, and the other scaly creatures you will meet in this book, and they are the REPTILES! The dictionary says the word *reptile* comes from an old Latin word for "creeping" (not "creepy"). These creepers are the cold-blooded creatures that thrive in the warm regions across the middle of our globe. Reptiles claim territory in North America, South America, Europe, Asia, Africa, and Australia. They live on land in the tropics, the deserts, the prairies, and the woodlands. They live in fresh waters, murky swamps, and the salty seas. Just as we humans live all around the earth, so do the reptiles. The way they prefer to live is hidden, undisturbed by us. Now, curious reader, if you are fascinated by reptiles, read on! If you are maybe a little afraid of reptiles, read on! The scaly creatures in this book are real. They are more amazing than fantasy. And they are hidden in this book waiting for you to discover them!

In Chapter 1, you'll learn what makes reptiles special and different from all other living creatures. You will get the straight reptile story on two things that often confuse kids and adults. First, what does "cold-blooded" mean? Second, are lizards and salamanders the same? (Hint: No.)

Within the next four chapters you will discover four kinds of reptiles: snakes, lizards, turtles, and crocodilians. In Chapter 2 each species of snake you meet will teach you something about how snakes live. Chapter 3 puts the spotlight on several species of lizards that will show you how much variety there is in lizard life. The ways of turtles will be shown with the help of some spotlight species in Chapter 4. Finally, in Chapter 5 the spotlight will move to some crocodilians to introduce to you the last big group of reptiles.

Try This

At the Zoo, Compare a Reptile to You

Go to the zoo on a slow day, bring a pencil and a pad of paper, sit down near a display for a reptile, and make two lists. Look long and think hard about the scaly creature in front of you. List everything about it that makes it like you and everything that makes it different from you. Herpetologists learn a lot from long thoughtful observations.

WORDS to KNOW

PALEONTOLOGY: When you read about animals like dinosaurs that lived and died long ago, you are studying *paleontology*. Paleontologists can study fossils, bones, or prints left in stone. They do biology of the past. When you observe and study a living reptile, you are doing a biology of the present, *herpetology*.

By Chapter 6 you will be ready to take a sharper look at the reptiles and marvel at more of their *adaptations*. Do you know what that word means? The reptiles have some adaptations that are quite different from yours. Take your five (human) senses, for example, which you learned about when you were young. Reptile senses are different and quite interesting. And how would you behave if you were "cold-blooded"?

If you read all the way to Chapter 7 you will learn about the many stories people tell about reptiles. In many stories reptiles play the bad guys, but in some they play the good guys! In that chapter you will also learn about the bright people who study reptiles and what they are learning from these animals. You might even decide that they have a job you want some day!

As you read through this book, you're likely to have a favorite reptile. You might think, "I want one of those!" Chapter 8 gives you the important information needed for proper and safe care of reptilian pets. Remember, a family pet is a family decision; you want everyone to agree before you bring one home. Chapter 9 suggests and describes six reptile species that make good pets for beginners.

MEMBERS ONLY

To belong to the Reptile Club you have to be cold-blooded, breathe air, and have a backbone. This members list has got all jumbled. Can you figure out these 6 reptile names?

KESAN	STOOTIRE
RAZILD	CRIDELCOO
RUTTEL	GRALOLAIT

Chapter 1
Fascinating Reptiles

Things that are different from what you're familiar with can scare you or they can make you very, very curious. That is the cool thing about reptiles! They are certainly different from furry mammals. You are a mammal and so is a dog. Reptiles are not mammals. Petting a snake is not like petting a cat or a hamster. Lizards and turtles do not walk like squirrels, rabbits, or foxes. Alligators do not hunt like wolves. Reptiles have their own strange appearance and fascinating ways. When you begin to learn about them you learn what makes them special, but you can also learn what makes them similar to mammals and to you.

We Are the World! We Are Reptilian!

You might wonder how many reptiles are in the world. Counting each of them would be impossible, but scientists do count how many species of reptiles Earth has. Scientists are still finding new species they had never before counted. Scientists sometimes disagree on how many species there are, but a good guess right now is that there are 10,000 or more reptile species in the world. So let's meet the crowd.

The Tropics Are Rich in Reptiles

The best places on Earth to meet lots of reptiles are near the equator. Look at a globe of Earth. Pretend the North Pole is the head, the South Pole is the feet, and the equator is the belt around the middle. Land near Earth's equator holds amazing tropical habitats. Tropical habitats have warm, moist air and plants that grow all year long. Those special habitats are also home to many snakes, lizards, turtles, crocodiles, and alligators. All the things that reptiles need are there in the tropics: warmth from the sun, water, and food. Reptiles are easy to find in continents with tropical habitats. Africa is home to 1,650 reptile species. About 2,000 reptile species live in South America.

Reptiles Live Far and Wide and Nearby

Some rare species of reptiles live in only one small place—for instance, the Galapagos Islands, which are the only place in the world to find the marine iguanas. Other more common reptile species have habitats across many miles of land or sea. For example, adders are the only poisonous snakes in Europe, but adders also live across northern Asia all the way to its eastern side. Adder habitats are found on two continents!

Within the United States and Canada there live about 300 species of reptiles. You may or may not live in a place where scaly reptiles are seen as often as furry mammals, but on Earth the number of reptile species is nearly double the number of mammal species. The only continent where you cannot find living reptiles is Antarctica. You probably do not live there, so you should learn more about your scaly neighbors closer to home.

WORDS to KNOW

HABITAT: Every animal and plant needs a certain kind of place in which to live and grow. Each needs its habitat for food, water, and shelter. Studying one reptile's habitat means learning everything you can about the weather, plants, animals, and land around its little home. To protect reptiles, people protect the reptiles' habitats.

Reptiles Inside and Out

Bones and scales are two important things for describing all reptiles. First, reptiles have bones inside. Bones are what make reptiles like mammals but different from worms and giant squids. Second, reptiles have scales on the outside. Scales makes reptiles different from furry mammals and feathered birds.

A Skeleton on the Inside

Since reptiles have bones, reptiles are called *vertebrates*. All creatures called vertebrates are named after their most important bones, called *vertebrae*. Like a reptile, you have vertebrae in

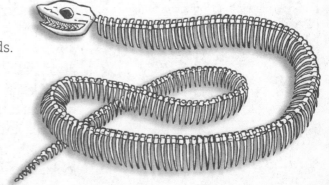

the middle of your back. You call them your backbone. Each piece of the backbone alone is called one *vertebra*. A vertebra has a hole like a donut. Running through the middle of each vertebra is a cord of nerves from the brain called the *spinal cord*. The vertebrae bones have two important jobs.

Two Important Things That Vertebrae Do for a Reptile

1. Each vertebra protects the spinal cord of nerves running from the brain. If that cord is hurt or cut, a reptile may not be able to send messages from its brain to its legs. The reptile would then be unable to move its legs.
2. Together, vertebrae are the main, middle piece holding together the rest of the skeleton inside a reptile.

Even though some reptiles have bone in the scales on the outside of their bodies, it is the bones on the inside of a reptile that hold it together and hold it up. Having vertebrae and other bones inside of you makes you similar to a reptile.

Covered in Fingernails?

Scales make reptiles look and feel very different than other animals. Reptiles have scales for many reasons. Scales are the armor of a reptile when it battles for food. Scales make a perfect raincoat for a reptile, since scales are quite waterproof. Scales are also the wall that holds in moisture to keep a reptile from drying out.

How a reptile grows its scales is neat. They are made of something called *keratin*, which is like the plastic that people use to make tools and toys. Reptiles and other vertebrate creatures naturally make keratin in their bodies. Keratin is a strong and flexible protein. While some proteins help build strong muscles (your parents may have told you that at the dinner table), keratin builds other handy body parts: claws, fingernails, fur, feathers, hair, horns, skin, and scales. So feel a fingernail and think of it as a big scale. Feel a snake or lizard and think of them as covered with tiny fingernails.

Like animals in their variety of fur coats and people in their variety of hairstyles, reptiles also have a variety of looks because of their different kinds of scales.

Reptile Scales Can Be Very Different!

- Some scales overlap to make a reptile smooth.
- Some scales form spikes on a reptile to make it look big and scary.
- Some scales are small like tiny beads or grains of sand.
- Some scales are like large plates of armor.
- Some are keeled, meaning that they have ridges.
- Some, called *osteoderms*, have bone inside to make them strong.

Some scales have special uses. For example, snakes have special scales on their bellies called *ventral scales* and a rattlesnake's rattle is made of scales.

No Central Heating

Reptiles are called "cold-blooded" creatures. People and other mammals are called "warm-blooded." Those words are confusing. Here is why. You have a normal body temperature of about 98.6 degrees Fahrenheit. If your body's temperature changes, that means you are sick. Some people mistake the way reptile bodies work. Some people assume reptile bodies work like yours except at a lower temperature with colder blood. That is not what cold-blooded means. Reptiles do not have cold blood.

When They're Hot They're Hot.
When They're Cold They're Cold.

What really makes reptiles different is how they heat their bodies. Think of a mammal's body as a house with a heater inside and an air conditioner too. When it's cold outside, a mammal's body works and uses energy to make its own heat. Mammals also cool themselves when it is hot outside. For example, you sweat to keep cool. When the air dries sweat off your skin, you cool off. A reptile cannot do that. Think of a reptile's body as a house with no heater or air conditioner inside.

Instead of heating from the inside, reptiles get heat from the sun. The temperature of a reptile's

Nope, Not a Reptile!

Does an armadillo have scales? No, armadillos are covered in bony shell and a wee bit of hair. Reptiles are hairless. Also, armadillos have big cute ears, and reptile ears look just like holes or circles on the sides of their heads. The armadillo is a mammal, not a reptile.

It's getting cold out and this snake has to find shelter or he will freeze. Luckily he can read the reptile code. Can you figure it out too?

CODE FOR THE COLD

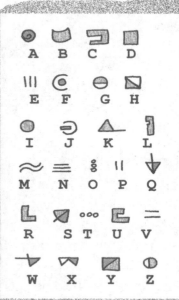

A	B	C	D
E	F	G	H
I	J	K	L
M	N	O	P	Q
R	S	T	U	V
W	X	Y	Z

WARM BODIED

We use up large amounts of energy keeping our body temperature the same so we eat lots of food. Snakes can go for weeks without food because they are not using up energy regulating their body temperatures.

body goes up and down when the temperature outside goes up and down. When the weather gets too hot, a reptile must find someplace cooler. When the weather cools, a reptile must find a place to stay warm.

If you go outside in the sunny summer and the temperature is 102 degrees Fahrenheit, you may feel hot but you can keep your body temperature at 98.6 degrees for quite a while. When a lizard goes out into 102-degree heat, it will not take long for its body temperature to reach 102 degrees. The same is true for a cool cloudy day in the fall. You can run around with no jacket, and your body temperature will not drop. A reptile cannot wear a jacket nor stop its body temperature from dropping. This is very important to know about reptiles, and this explains why they do not live in Antarctica!

Sorry, No Frogs in This Book

Squishy frogs, salamanders, toads, newts, and mudpuppies are vertebrates just like reptiles but they are not scaly creatures. They are amphibians. A tiger salamander and a leopard gecko may have similar sizes, shapes, and spots, but only the gecko is a reptile. Some people may confuse you when they call salamanders "spring lizards." The common names we use for creatures often describe what the animal looks like, but not what it really is. Make no mistake—reptiles and amphibians are related, but they are not the same. Here are some reasons why.

WORDS to KNOW

HERPETOLOGISTS:
Scientists who study reptiles and amphibians are called *herpetologists*. A herpetologist might say "That's a fine-looking herp!" when discovering a bullfrog or a bull snake in a swamp. Herpetologists call all reptiles and amphibians herps.

A FEW DIFFERENCES BETWEEN REPTILES AND AMPHIBIANS

REPTILES	AMPHIBIANS
MANY REPTILES EAT AMPHIBIANS.	AMPHIBIANS RARELY EAT REPTILES.
REPTILES LIKE LIZARDS, TURTLES, AND ALLIGATORS HAVE CLAWS.	AMPHIBIANS HAVE NO REAL CLAWS.
REPTILES HAVE DRY, SCALY, WATERPROOF SKIN.	AMPHIBIANS HAVE MOIST, SENSITIVE SKIN.

That last difference is important. Sure, reptiles may get just as wet and muddy as frogs or salamanders, but amphibian skin cannot get as dry as reptile skin. Amphibian skin also has less keratin. This allows amphibians to breathe in oxygen through their skin, but it also makes the skin more sensitive and fragile. Reptiles can only breathe in oxygen with their lungs (as you do), so they can grow tougher skin. This skin allows them to spend more time in the sunlight and to live and creep in places where amphibians cannot. Some reptiles live in deserts and some live in salt water, both places where amphibians could not survive. You might say that reptiles and amphibians are distant cousins and reptiles are the tougher cousins.

Reptiles in Ponds Are Still Reptiles

You may have read that amphibians are cold-blooded creatures that "live part of their lives in the water." Sometimes people hear that and think turtles are amphibians because they live in ponds and swamps like frogs do. However, many reptiles also spend part of the day in the water hunting, hiding, or cooling off. Some reptiles spend most of their lives in the water! Some live in the ocean. Dig deeper to understand. The key to this problem is when reptiles spend time in the water and when amphibians spend time in water. An important clue is what time of day the animal is in the water.

Baby Reptiles versus Baby Amphibians

You can often tell a reptile from an amphibian at the beginning of its life. Reptiles often begin life on land and amphibians must begin life somewhere in water. Reptiles that do lay eggs go to dry land and lay them. Amphibians must lay their eggs in water. Life for baby reptiles is different than life for baby amphibians.

DIFFERENCES BETWEEN REPTILE AND AMPHIBIAN LIFE CYCLES

REPTILES	AMPHIBIANS
REPTILE EGGS USUALLY HAVE LEATHERY SHELLS.	AMPHIBIAN EGGS ARE JELLY-COATED.
REPTILES CAN LAY THEIR EGGS ON LAND BECAUSE THAT LEATHERY SHELL KEEPS THEM FROM DRYING OUT.	AMPHIBIANS MUST LAY THEIR JELLY-COATED EGGS IN FRESH WATER BECAUSE THOSE EGGS WOULD DIE ON DRY LAND.
REPTILE BABIES ARE NORMALLY LITTLE COPIES OF THEIR PARENTS.	AMPHIBIAN BABIES GO THROUGH GREAT CHANGES BEFORE THEY LOOK LIKE THEIR ADULT PARENTS.
REPTILE BABIES AND ADULTS ALWAYS BREATHE WITH LUNGS AS YOU DO.	AMPHIBIAN BABIES MAY BREATHE FOR SOME TIME WITH GILLS LIKE FISH INSTEAD OF LUNGS.

Some reptiles give birth to babies live, and almost all amphibians lay eggs. Whether a reptile is hatched or born, it comes out of its mother looking very much like her. Each one is Mom's little Mini-Me! You might already know that female frogs lay eggs that become tadpoles with tails. The tadpoles look more like fish than frogs. That's how it is with amphibians; most go through great changes as they grow to adults. But as reptile babies grow bigger, their bodies make much smaller changes, like changes to the color of their skin.

Reptiles Go Way Back to the Dino Days

When you look at an iguana or a crocodile, you cannot help but think of dinosaurs and imagine a time millions of years ago when reptiles ruled the whole world. That was the time when species like the Spinosaurus, Stegosaurus, and Tyrannosaurus rex lived. In fact the word *dinosaur* comes from ancient Greek words meaning "terrifying lizard." Scientists are still trying to figure out how today's reptiles are related to the dinosaurs. It is amazing to think that when the dinosaurs lived, during what some people call the "Age of Reptiles," the world was the very opposite of today. Back then many reptiles were huge, and beneath them little furry mammals scurried on the ground. Today people and many mammals are big while the reptiles creeping on the ground are mostly small.

You Learned a Lot from What Reptiles Are Not

Someone may learn a lot about you when you say "I am not like my brother" or "I am not like my sister." Hopefully, you have already learned a lot about reptiles by learning why they are neither mammals nor amphibians. But reptiles are not completely different from other creatures. Like amphibians, and like you and other mammals, they have bones, blood, and skin.

TERRIFYING LIZARD*

These animals were around millions of years ago and are directly related to reptiles. Can you tell what they are? To find out, complete the rows of 3-letter words, then read the middle letters from top to bottom.

A __ D
P __ N
I __ K
S __ N
A __ K
P __ T
R __ N
A __ M

WHY DID THE TWO BOA CONSTRICTORS GET MARRIED?

What's another name for "terrifying lizard"? Answer in the back of the book.

Chapter 2

First Let's Take the Snakes

Pretending to change into a snake is a good way to learn how snakes live and move. So imagine. First, your arms and legs have got to go! Next, you will need a forked tongue. (That means it's split in two at the tip.) Then, you must do something about your backbone. You need a lot more vertebrae to be a snake! As a human you have thirty-three, but as a snake you could have one hundred eighty or even four hundred vertebrae. Your human ribs come in twelve pairs connected to the vertebrae below your neck. They make a big cage to protect your heart and lungs. As a snake you would have more than one hundred pairs of ribs forming a narrow tunnel to protect your insides.

Do the Locomotion

A snake's vertebrae make it able to move differently than a simple spineless worm. Watch a worm and it seems, without folding or bending, to stretch and squish itself as it travels on the dirt. Snakes are shaped like worms but they are more complicated. Snakes travel on land, water, and trees. Some snakes can even jump and sail through the air! How they move is fun to observe. Below are names for special kinds of snake locomotion.

Four Far-Out Snake Locomotions
1. Serpentine, a common slither
2. Sidewinding, a cool desert run
3. Concertina, an accordion-style step
4. Rectilinear, a straight line crawl

You will understand these methods of moving and grooving as you meet some snakes from near and far. The first snakes you meet will be quite typical or average snakes. Then you will meet the snakes with poisonous bites and the snakes with powerful hugs. All of them have interesting snake anatomy to teach you.

Some Snakes Are So Typical

Snakes are usually small. Most snakes are not much longer than an adult human's arm. Most snakes tend to live near a supply of water. Most snakes of North America are not poisonous or deadly. Most hunt small prey. Read on and get to know some snakes that are typical in these ways. You will also begin to learn how snakes eat their prey.

I Found a Garter Snake!

That's what people are likely to say in North America if they find a snake. Garters live across the United States and Canada. If you have found one yourself, you might be surprised to know that yours is not the only kind of garter. There are more than a dozen species of garter. Most garter species are about two feet long. The species called the common garter hunts amphibians, small fish, and insects. For the species called the plains garter, frogs are the favorite food. Since garters are small, slow to bite, and not poisonous, they are quite harmless to you. A garter is a good snake to know because it is very typical of snakes in general.

Most garter snakes wear a friendly face with large, smart-looking eyes above a mouth that seems to smile. They have dark round pupils in their eyes. Many garters wear stripes that run from head to tail. The plains garter has plain-looking stripes. Its body is black and the stripe down its back is yellow. Down each side of it runs a pale stripe, nothing fancy. However, some garter snakes are snazzier. The checkered garter wears (you guessed it) a checkerboard pattern instead of stripes.

Garter snakes live in many places: in prairies, in ditches, near lakes, near ponds, in swamps, and often in the shady

WORDS to KNOW

PREY: Many reptiles hunt and eat small animals. The animals that reptiles eat are called their *prey*. Prey can also mean "to hunt and eat." You can say some snakes prey on frogs. It is not right to say iguanas prey on leaves, because they do not sneak up on leaves before they eat them.

FUN FACT

Why Call It a Garter?
Some kids spot them in the garden and call them "gardener snakes" but the common name is garter. A garter is something men used to wear to hold up their black socks. Whoever named garter snakes thought they looked like little sock suspenders!

grass of a backyard. Some have done well living near people. If you spot one making its way along the ground, you'll find it cool to watch. The garter will show you one of the four far-out ways that snakes move.

Garters often move in the serpentine way. To picture serpentine locomotion, draw the letter S. While moving in an S shape each curve of the garter's body pushes it along. The sides of its body can push off of the grass and other things that stick up from the ground.

Garters hunt during the day. Since they do not poison or hug their prey to death, they must strike fast and swallow critters alive. The plains garter tries to swallow frogs head first. Do frogs talk too much if they are swallowed feet first? No. The slimy thing fits inside the garter's mouth much better with the head first. That way the frog's legs get pressed against its sides. Many snakes, especially those that eat large prey, follow the "eat 'em head first" rule. Parts like claws or hooves can hurt or even puncture a big snake if they're swallowed first. Eating is slow and careful business for snakes. No fast food!

Hognose, Typical but Different

The eastern hognose snake and its cousins, the western hognose and the southern hognose, are also basically harmless North American snakes. They also are about two feet or more in length, but they're much pudgier than the garters. A hognose hunts small prey—it digs to find the tasty toads. It has brown blotches on its back and a short skinny tail. Its best feature is the sharp upturned scale in the middle of its face, which makes it look a bit like a pig. A hognose can shovel dirt like a pig digs with its nose. When a hognose digs out a toad, it must strike quickly and, of course, swallow the toad whole.

Dinner Time Again, and Look Mom No Hands!

How do garters, hognoses, and other snakes shove prey into their mouths whole without forks, fingers, or hands? They do it with a jaw that works in ways yours cannot. Try moving your jaw right now in all the ways you can. Your lower jawbone can move on its hinges up and down to chomp, chomp, chomp. It can also move side to side to help you chew, chew, chew. Snakes can do much more. A snake's upper and lower jaw bones can unhinge and stretch far apart. A snake's upper jaw bones can also split into halves (left and right). Each half pokes at the prey to push it down into the throat. This is a lot of work for a snake and takes some time. If you had a whole double cheeseburger stuck in your mouth for that long, you would have trouble breathing. But for a snake, that is not a problem. Ask a snake to say "Ahh" and you'll see something special. Most snakes have a breathing tube at the bottom of their mouth. It can extend out from underneath their prey while they work to swallow it.

Hognose Has Big Back Teeth

Some of the tasty toads that a hognose likes to eat can make themselves into a mouthful when bitten. Some toads puff themselves up to keep from going down a snake's throat. But a hognose can pop them (gross, sorry) with two larger teeth in the back of its mouth. Those two teeth are fangs. A hognose works those rear fangs in while getting a good hold on its prey. What goes in with the fangs is some

WORDS to KNOW

SCIENTIFIC NAME: Herpetologists have a special name for the eastern hognose, *Heterodon platirhinos*. Those are Latin words that mean "different teeth" and "flat nose." Every reptile has a fancy scientific name.

TryThis

Saliva, More Than Just for Spitting!

Put a soda cracker into your mouth. Chew it, but do not swallow. First it tastes salty. Keep chewing slowly without swallowing. The salty taste goes away and the cracker mush begins to taste slightly sweet because your saliva begins to digest (break down, or change) the cracker's starches into sugar. The poison in a hognose's saliva is also meant for breaking down its food.

TASTY TREATS

Don't kill snakes. If they were gone they wouldn't eat animals that can cause us harm. Can you figure out what snakes like to eat?

Change one letter in **Cats** to get a tasty snake treat.

Add one letter to **Nails** to get a favorite for some snakes.

Add a letter to **Fog** to get a nutritious snack.

Change a letter in **Shake** to get a surprise favorite.

Change a letter in **House** to get a tasty snack.

MMMM, DINNER!

Snakes are found around the world. They eat many things including crayfish, grasshoppers, skinks, and spiders. Mmmmm!

saliva. That saliva has poison. This seems fair, since some toads that hognoses eat have mild poison of their own in their skin.

A bite from a hognose is not considered poisonous enough to call dangerous, unlike bites from the snakes you will read about later. A bite from a hognose (which doesn't usually bite) could hurt and might cause some swelling, but it will not kill a person. Other species of snakes have rear fangs like the hognose; however, only a very few of them are dangerous. One of those few lives in the trees of southern Africa. It is the extremely dangerous boomslang. It may have big eyes and a smile like a garter snake, but don't be fooled. Its bite is deadly. Still, to understand who the poisonous snakes are, you must get to know the fellas with their fangs in the front.

Some Are Poisonous

Almost all dangerously poisonous snakes have front fangs. That means two fangs in the front of the upper jaw with no teeth in between. Two snake families have these front fangs. The first is the rattlesnakes and their relatives. The second is the cobras and their cousins. These two families look different and bite differently, but both families deserve respect and safe distance. Read on, meet them, and learn more about snake fangs, movement, and digestion.

Beware the Viper Gang

Rattlesnakes are the rock stars of the viper gang. If you are hiking in the dry lands of the western United States, you may hear a western diamondback rattlesnake making what sounds like the fast music of a maraca. The diamondback is shaking the rattle at the end of its tail. If you are in the hills or prairie woodlands of the eastern United States, you may hear the timber rattlesnake play its rattle. Do not stay for the concert. The rattlers are telling you to keep away.

A safer place to see a rattlesnake is behind glass in a zoo. There you may see that rattlers are short and thick like a hognose. Most vipers are built short in the body but long in the fangs. Vipers also have a large triangle-shaped head. North American rattlers often have keeled scales that feel rough. They have dull shades of gray, dark brown, or tan. They often have large-shaped patterns on their backs.

In the Mojave Desert in California and Nevada lives a rattlesnake with visors like a horn above each eye. Some people call it the horned rattlesnake. It has rough scales that shape patterns, but a more curious pattern lies in the tracks it leaves in the sand dunes. Before the hot wind blows them away you might spy the tracks. They look like a young child's tally marks trailing off diagonally across the desert.

This night-hunting snake moves strangely because the sand is too loose for it to move in the serpentine way like the garter does. Instead, it goes forward and sideways at the same time while pressing one loop of its body down on the sand and throwing a second loop ahead. Each loop spreads the snake's weight straight down across the ground, keeping it on top of the loose sand. This is sidewinding, and this rattler is commonly called the sidewinder. Now you know the second of the four far-out snake locomotions. The sidewinder's way of running on sand is smart, for if you ever took a long walk on a sandy beach in your bare feet you know it is not easy.

Rattlers are not the only vipers. Some other North American vipers have no toys on their tails but still have large triangle-shaped heads. One of them can hide among dry leaves in states near and east of the Mississippi River. That's the copperhead. It is about three feet long. Another common viper is a water moccasin. It seems strange to name a snake after a wet shoe! Instead some people call it the cottonmouth. In a pond or river you may see its head

TryThis

FuN FacT

Natural Swimmers

Many snakes can swim. In fact, many snakes are faster in the water.

A hot dog vendor sees a rattlesnake sidewinding down the street. He says to the snake, "Hey, you want a hot dog?" What does the snake say?

Answer: "No thanksssss, maybe jussssst a sssssausage or a FANGfurter."

above water as it swims across in the same serpentine way that works so well on land.

Poison is one reason a viper has a large head. The two glands that make and store poison begin inside its head. A viper has one such gland behind each eye right above the upper jaw. Snake poison is called *venom*. Snakes did not develop venom to kill people. It is meant for hunting and feeding, and snakes are serious about not wasting it. Venomous snakes do not eat people, so they would prefer not to use their venom on you. But beware of young little vipers; they are more wasteful with venom than the adults.

How front-fanged snakes work is amazing. Each fang is like a doctor's syringe. When you get a measles shot, a syringe squeezes vaccine through a hollow needle into your arm. Then it flows with your blood throughout your body. That is an injection. Front fangs are hollow and they too make injections. (Hopefully this won't make you afraid of shots!) When a viper bites its prey, it squeezes venom through its fangs into the prey. That means a diamondback rattlesnake will bite a rat, kill it, and then swallow it. That's different from a garter snake, which must swallow live frogs.

The cobras and their cousins also have hollow fangs, but vipers have bigger ones with two handy features. First, viper fangs fold back against the roof of the mouth when not in use but come down and hold still when striking. Without foldable fangs a viper could not close its mouth. Second, venom is precious to vipers and they control whether or not to inject it with each strike of their fangs. They may defend themselves without loosing venom.

After all this you may wish wild places had no vipers. The truth is that vipers do important work in their habitats. Vipers are great hunters of rodents like rats, mice, and rabbits. Those animals would increase to troublesome numbers if rattlers and their relatives did not hunt them. Sure, some people hate rattlers, but would they enjoy lots of rats?

Please Stay Away from the Elapids

The second group of front-fanged snakes is the elapids. Elapids have smaller heads and jaws that do not open as wide as the big-mouth vipers' jaws. Many elapids eat prey that fits quite well into their mouths. Many of them eat snakes. That seems pretty smart. If you're a snake, what could be easier to eat than a smaller snake? The elapids include the cobra and its cousins. Many elapids live along with vipers in Africa and Asia, but Australia's front-fangers are all elapids. Elapids also have some special habitats where vipers cannot be found. If you get to know some elapid species you will understand them better.

Elapids have shorter fangs but many elapids have much longer bodies than vipers. The king cobra is the royal example of this. Imagine a thirteen-foot-long snake that can raise its head and look at an adult person eye to eye. That is the king cobra. King cobras and some other cobras have a handy feature in their fangs that vipers might envy. They use their fangs like dual squirt guns for spraying venom. Through holes in the front of their fangs instead of the bottom they shoot venom at predators.

Herpetologists say it is not easy deciding what snake is the world's most poisonous. However, certainly many of the most deadly snakes are elapids. One is the tiger snake, named after the stripes that many snakes of the species wear. Its venom contains two kinds of poison, blood poison and nerve poison. Blood poisons attack blood and break down prey's muscles and skin. Nerve poisons attack nerves and work to stop the breathing and heart pumping in prey. Many elapids have very powerful nerve poisons, or neurotoxins.

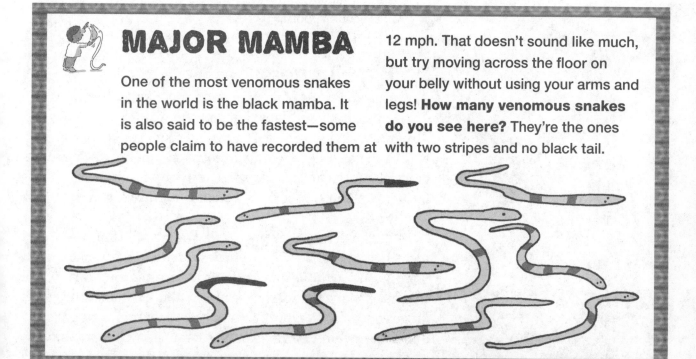

MAJOR MAMBA

One of the most venomous snakes in the world is the black mamba. It is also said to be the fastest—some people claim to have recorded them at 12 mph. That doesn't sound like much, but try moving across the floor on your belly without using your arms and legs! **How many venomous snakes do you see here?** They're the ones with two stripes and no black tail.

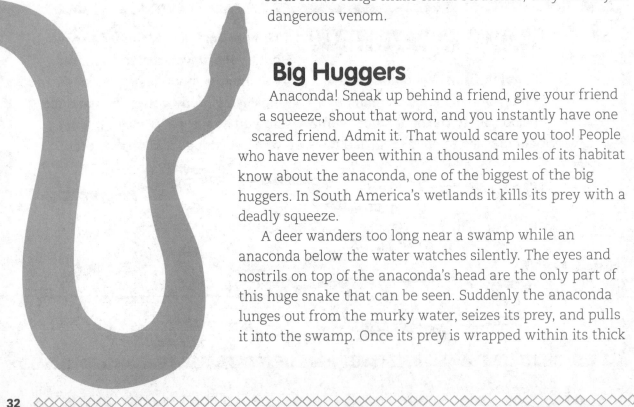

What Makes Food Go to a Snake's Stomach?

Muscles send food to the stomach. Neither a snake nor you needs to stand up straight and drop food to the stomach. To prove it, fill a paper cup with cold water. Ask a friend to hold you in a headstand against a wall. Use a straw to drink your water upside down. You and a snake both have muscles that push your food and water to your stomach.

Some elapids live in trees. The green mamba of West Africa is colored well for hunting among the leaves. Its slim body can grow to more than six feet long, so it can flow from branch to branch while hunting for birds. Africa's black mamba spends more time on the ground than the green mamba. It may be the world's fastest snake on land. It can zoom short distances at twelve miles per hour (that is fast for a snake). Never mess with the mambas. They are dangerous.

Some elapids live in the ocean. The olive sea snake hunts fish in the Pacific coast of Australia. It swims well with a long flattened body and a tail like a canoe paddle. Most sea snakes are very poisonous. However, the turtle-headed sea snake eats only fish eggs. It has no venom because it needs no venom to get its prey.

Fortunately the only elapids in North America are the western and eastern coral snakes. The red, yellow, and black rings on their small thirty-inch bodies are like a bright flag that says "danger." Harder to notice would be the marks left on a leg by a coral snake bite. But beware. Even though coral snake fangs make small scratches, they still inject dangerous venom.

Big Huggers

Anaconda! Sneak up behind a friend, give your friend a squeeze, shout that word, and you instantly have one scared friend. Admit it. That would scare you too! People who have never been within a thousand miles of its habitat know about the anaconda, one of the biggest of the big huggers. In South America's wetlands it kills its prey with a deadly squeeze.

A deer wanders too long near a swamp while an anaconda below the water watches silently. The eyes and nostrils on top of the anaconda's head are the only part of this huge snake that can be seen. Suddenly the anaconda lunges out from the murky water, seizes its prey, and pulls it into the swamp. Once its prey is wrapped within its thick

WIGGLY WAY OUT

These baby snakes have just been born. One little snake is packed and ready to see the world. But look at the maze he has to get through. Can you help him get out?

coils there is little chance for escape. Soon the anaconda is swallowing it whole.

Maybe this will sound less scary. While venomous snakes kill with their fangs, others kill with their coils. Coils are the loops a snake can wrap around its prey. If you have ever held a corn snake in your hands, then you know the muscle strength in a snake's coils. People across the country enjoy corn snakes as pets. Amazingly, a three-foot corn snake handles its prey in much the same way as the mighty anaconda, because it is a hugger too!

The huggers include two families plus many typical snakes like the corn snake. Two families of huggers are the boas of South America and the pythons of Africa, Asia, and Australia.

Get to Know Boas

The boas of South America include the anaconda. You may have heard of another called the boa constrictor, the

Who Wins the Biggest Snake Contest?

Anacondas may be the heaviest. Some have weighed over 300 pounds. The reticulated pythons might be the longest. Some have measured over twenty-six feet. But remember snakes stories are like fish stories. People tend to stretch them!

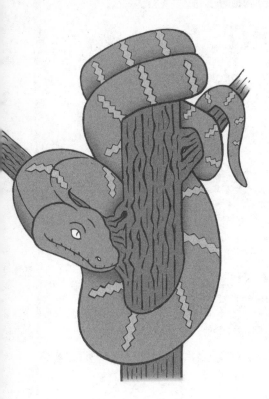

common boa. Its body can grow up to ten or more feet. Its head is large and narrow and ends in a square-looking snout.

The word "constrict" is an important word to know, because all the huggers are constrictors, not just the common boa. When the common boa puts the squeeze on its prey it does not kill by crushing bones. The boa constricts, or stops, its prey's breathing. Once a bird is in the boa's coils, the coils will tighten each time the bird breathes out, and soon the bird's lungs can breathe in no more air.

Many boas are thick and heavy, such as the emerald tree boa. It cannot flow across tree branches like the slender mambas. Instead it moves across branches folding and unfolding itself like an accordion. The emerald tree boa uses concertina movement. *Concertina* is an old word for the accordion. The emerald tree boa holds a branch with its tail end and reaches out for a hold with its head end. Then it folds itself up to bring its tail closer, and reaches out its head again to move farther.

Once Upon a Python

Another huge hugger is the reticulated python. It is big enough to eat almost anything, including you. Southeast Asia is where you may find it, or where you do not want it to find you.

After a reticulated python has swallowed a great meal, it follows the snake rule for eating: "Digest and rest." You may do that too on Thanksgiving, but for a python that has swallowed something with antlers, resting helps make sure it does not get hurt. After large meals all snakes can wait for a long time before the next meal.

When a snake grows as big as a reticulated python, it needs to use rectilinear locomotion. Most snakes can do it. They move like long muscular caterpillars along the ground. As they move, you can see a single wave of muscle movement from one end of the body to the other, much like seeing "the wave" move across the crowd in a sports stadium. The wave of motion pushes against the ground.

FUN FACT

Teeth That Hold

Pythons and many other snakes have teeth that point back into their mouths. This makes getting out of a snake's mouth very hard to do.

How the snake gets hold of the ground is also interesting. Flip any snake over and there is the secret. The smooth ventral scales running across a snake's belly can work like treads on car tires. Tire treads grab the road and push a car. That's what a snake's belly scales do.

Constrictors That May Be Close to Your Home

Many snakes related to the garter and the hognose are also constrictors. Their hugs pose no danger to you but will work on their prey. Besides the corn snake, these include the milk snake, the bull snake, the king snake, and others. Common king snakes live across the United States. They are usually black with pale rings and grow to more than three feet long. The common king snakes are also snake eaters. They are immune to rattler venom and can eat rattlesnakes for lunch.

Snake and Lizards, a Very Big Order!

All snakes use super-flexible jaws to eat live prey. Venomous snakes use fangs to inject venom. Constrictors use their coils to stop the breathing of their prey. All snakes use one or more of the four methods for getting around. That may seem like the whole snake story, but there are many other snakes besides the ones described here so far. Learning about reptiles always leads to surprises.

A Mysterious Snake Secret

If you want to learn something strange about snakes, go to a pet store that has snakes and an owner who knows about them. Ask the owner to show you the toes on a boa or a python. Yes, a ball python might be a good snake to look at. Underneath the snake near the start of its tail you can see what looks like a left and a right toe claw. These are called *spurs*, and they are clues. They lead herpetologists to believe, based on the tiny leftovers of legs, that snakes long ago used to crawl like lizards.

FUN FACT

Stretchable Jaws

Many snakes can eat prey three times bigger than their heads because of stretchy connections between their jaw bones.

Reptiles with Common Ancestors

The clue of the leftover legs leads herpetologists to look for other clues. Skulls of lizards and snakes give them more clues that snakes and lizards came from common ancestors long ago. For that reason herpetologists put snakes and lizards together in a bigger group called *Squamata*. That means "scaly ones."

Snake scales and lizard scales both look very different from turtle and crocodilian scales. Snakes and lizards also shed their skin all at once or in big pieces. Both grow new skin beneath the old first. A snake breaks its old skin at its nose then rubs and crawls out of it. A lizard's old skin peels off in chunks. Some lizards eat it for protein. (Yuck.) Shed skin of snakes and lizards is almost see-through and lighter than tissue paper.

TryThis

Take Off Your Socks and Learn

Watch as you take off your socks. What happens to them? They end up inside out. If you are lucky enough to find a whole shed snake skin, remember that it is inside out too.

Be a Snake Helper

Snakes are super survivors but many of them could need help. For instance, California has two garter snakes in trouble. The garter snakes that live in wetlands near San Francisco have a beautiful combination of red and black stripes with pale blue-green stripes that make them unique. Those wetlands are the only place they live and many of those wetlands are being changed or destroyed by people. California's giant garter snake is also losing its wetland habitats. The giant garter is unique for its size. Imagine a garter snake that can grow five feet long!

If you want to help snakes, there are things you can do.

Get to Know the Habitats Near You

Where are the wild areas in your part of the country? Find out which snakes live there. Learn what you can about them. It's easy—you've already started reading about snakes. When you and the adults in your life know who your reptile neighbors are and learn about them, you will probably want to protect them.

GREEN GARDEN GIFT

One of the best ways to help snakes is to give them places to live. If you have a yard, ask your parents about setting aside an area as a wild garden. The snakes will find their way to it soon enough. There are 13 snakes hidden in the foliage of this garden—can you spot them?

CALL A DOCTOR!

WHAT DO YOU GIVE A SICK SNAKE?

Practice Safety When Hiking

Think safety instead of fear. Fear of snakes still leads many kids and adults to unnecessarily kill snakes. Most snake are harmless, but the number of people who die from snakebite in the United States in a year is about ten. Learn which poisonous snakes live in your part of the country and learn where their habitats are. Leave the searching for poisonous snakes to professional herpetologists. If you are hiking with your family in a place far from home, listen when local people tell you about poisonous snakes in the places you visit. For example, if you are vacationing in the Badlands of South Dakota and see a "Beware Rattlesnakes" sign, do not go searching for a chance to see a prairie rattlesnake. Finally, follow the rules below.

Safety Tips to Prevent Snake Bites When Hiking

- Wear boots.
- Hike with an adult, or in groups.
- Stay on the trails made for you.
- Carrying a walking stick is fun. If you must poke in holes or cracks, use your stick, not your hand.

SCIENTIFIC NAMES FOR SNAKES

COMMON NAME	SCIENTIFIC NAME
COMMON GARTER	THAMNOPHIS SIRTALIS
PLAINS GARTER	THAMNOPHIS RADIX
BOOMSLANG	DISPHOLIDUS TYPUS
WESTERN DIAMONDBACK RATTLESNAKE	CROTALUS ATROX
TIMBER RATTLESNAKE	CROTALUS HORRIDUS
SIDEWINDER	CROTALUS CERASTES
ANACONDA	EUNECTES MURINUS

Chapter 3
Lots of Kinds of Lizards

Among reptiles, lizards rule! They may not be as long as anacondas, big as crocodiles, nor cute as turtles, but lizards beat all other reptiles with numbers and variety. Some herpetologists have counted up to five thousand species of lizards! That is more than snake, turtle, and crocodilian species combined. When you say lizards have variety, that means they come in many kinds: huge, tiny, plain, fancy, prickly, smooth, harmless, or poisonous. How can you begin to learn about lizards? First, begin with the lizard basics. You learned that snakes and lizards are related. Now learn what makes lizards special. Then meet the iguanas and lizards like them called the *iguania* or *iguanians*. Use your imagination again as you read.

TryThis

Measure a Reptile

When you measure a reptile, measure it from the tip of its head to the tip of its tail. Don't try learning this with an alligator. Instead trying measuring a friend's pet lizard or ask a pet store owner to show you how. A lizard's tail is often as long as, or a wee bit longer than, its body.

Lizard Basics and Fancy Lizards

Imagine you are walking through a sandy field somewhere in Wisconsin. You spy what appears to be a three-foot snake catching a big June bug. Something about its face seems weird. It blinks and looks down at the grass without moving its head. That's it! Snakes cannot blink or move their eyes. This is a western slender glass lizard! That species is rare and this one is big!

What Makes Lizards So Special?

The slender glass lizard is not the only species of legless lizard. There are many other such species. This is confusing, and you may wonder why a legless lizard is not called a snake. The truth is, "legs or no legs" is not the surest way to tell a lizard apart from a snake.

HOW ARE LIZARDS AND SNAKES DIFFERENT?

LIZARDS	SNAKES
LIZARDS HAVE EARS THAT YOU CAN SEE.	YOU WILL NEVER SEE EARS ON A SNAKE.
LIZARDS HAVE EYELIDS.	SNAKES HAVE NO EYELIDS.
LIZARDS HAVE EYES THAT MOVE AROUND WELL.	SNAKE EYES DO NOT MOVE.
SOME LIZARDS EAT PLANTS.	SNAKES ONLY EAT ANIMALS, USUALLY FRESH. YOU WILL NEVER HEAR A SNAKE ORDER A SALAD.
LIZARDS USUALLY HAVE LONG TAILS.	SNAKES MAY HAVE LONG BODIES, BUT THEIR TAILS ARE SHORTER.
LIZARDS DO NOT HAVE VENTRAL SCALES ON THEIR BELLIES.	SNAKES DO.

Every great herpetologist marvels at a lizard she has never seen before. Every species has things that make it unique and things that make it similar to others. Lizards have their own ways of moving on the ground, in the water, through the trees, and through the air. Lizards have developed cool ways to find food. Lizards have curious things you can discover about their anatomy.

Cool Features in Lizards
- Their tails
- Their tongues
- Their legs
- Their decorations

Different lizard tongues grow in special shapes for different uses. Some lizards use theirs like harpoons! Lizard tails, whether long or short, are also very important. A lizard may use it as a whip, a hand, a balance pole, or an escape trick. Legs with claws are used a lot by lizards running, climbing, or digging. And last, some lizards can be very decorated with frills, horns, hoods, and beards. On lizards those decorations are not just extras—they have uses! Meet the iguanas first and learn how.

The Famous Iguanas

Suppose you are traveling the Pacific Ocean in a boat on the west side of South America. About 600 miles away from Ecuador, your boat's captain announces that you may now visit "the park." You wonder where the playground is, but you have only arrived at some rocky islands. This is the park: Ecuador's Galapagos National Park. It is a protected home for some rare species found nowhere else on Earth. Among these rare animals you can see two species of Galapagos land iguanas.

A Galapagos land iguana is a chubby lizard with a lumpy face and a fat head. Like most lizards, it walks with its legs spread out on both sides of its body, not under it like a four-legged mammal. Like most lizards, it has four legs with five toes on each foot.

However, some park visitors are surprised to see these three-foot-long reptiles eating plants. In fact when full-grown they eat mostly cactuses and weigh up to twenty-eight pounds! While watching one iguana scratch thorns off a cactus leaf you may see it nod its head at another that wanders in. He is not agreeing with the new guy. Nodding is a display that a male iguana uses to tell another male "This is my territory."

The islands are made of volcanic lava turned to stone, and not many plants grow there. So a third iguana species must find different food. They are the marine iguanas. Most marine iguanas eat algae from the seawater caught in pools along the rocky shore. Imagine a shore with forty or more iguanas grazing and lounging. It looks like a bizarre lizard vacation resort! The largest iguanas on the beach do leave shore and dive deep into the ocean to eat seaweed. They can hold their breath for as long as ten minutes while diving.

FuN FACT

Darwin Did Not Think They Were Cute

Charles Darwin wrote a book called *The Origin of Species*. After visiting the iguanas on the Galapagos Islands in 1835, he said they looked "disgusting." However, he noticed that they had adapted to their island by learning to swim and dive for food. Other iguanas don't do that.

WORDS to KNOW

YOU ARE WHAT YOU EAT: *Carnivores* eat animals. *Herbivores* are plant eaters. Some iguanas eat both, so they are *omnivores*.

The marine and land iguanas on Galapagos both have one long row of spines down the middle of the neck and back. That decoration likely makes them look bigger, and looking bigger helps a lizard survive. The land iguana, however, is larger. The marine iguana has a shorter snout and flatter tail. That means its tail is shaped like a sea snake's body. When marine iguanas or any iguanas swim, they move their bodies and tails in the same serpentine way that a sea snake does when it swims. Many iguanas are excellent swimmers. In fact, herpetologists guess that Galapagos and other islands have iguanas today because long ago some survived accidents that sent them out to sea.

The Galapagos iguanas are famous, but they are not the only iguanas. If you left Galapagos and came ashore to South America, you could find another big species. The green iguana lives among lush green trees in habitats across the continent. They eat leaves and flowers. They like to live near water, because swimming is their great escape when predators come too close.

If a green iguana cannot escape to the water or up a tree, it must run. Fortunately many iguanas are good runners. When they run, their tails become very important. The weight of a lizard's tail keeps its body from lurching too much with each stride. Without a tail, a running lizard's weight would be imbalanced to one side or another. With a tail, a running lizard holds its center of gravity.

A green iguana's face looks more like a fire-breathing dragon than a leaf-eating lizard. It has large eyes that watch its surroundings very closely. It has a large mouth. Above each corner of its mouth are round, flat ears. A male iguana has below its chin a beard of loose skin, called a *dewlap*. This decoration is for the head-nodding or head-bobbing display that iguanas do. When the green iguana raises itself high on its four legs and flaps its dewlap like a flag, it looks bigger

FUN FACT

No Sweat!

Marine iguanas often have chalky white faces. That is salt. Their bodies collect a lot of salt from the food they eat. Your body can sweat out extra salt. An iguana's body cannot. No sweat—they just sneeze it out. But you can plainly see they don't use a hanky!

and fiercer. Reptile expert Melissa Kaplan thinks another decoration is also interesting. The green iguana has a huge round scale below each corner of its mouth. She thinks that scale looks like a big scary eye when the dewlap is flapped. That may scare a few predators.

A green iguana's length can be more than five feet, but describing its color is not so easy. Describing a mammal's color can be complicated if its fur changes with the seasons of the year. Iguanas' color changes are even more complicated depending where the iguana lives or what the temperature is. Other iguanians, not just iguanas, also do amazing color changing. So, the green iguana is not always green. Sometimes it is greenish tan, or a bit blue, or even orange. It often has dark stripes on its tail.

If there is any confusion with its common name, there is no trouble with the green iguana's simple scientific name, *Iguana iguana*. All other iguanas and iguanians get their name from the green iguana. It's a classic!

Not Iguana-Wannabes—They Are Iguanians

Many lizard species share similar features with iguanas. Many of them are small. Anoles are some of those little iguanians. They live across South America and into North America. These pocket-sized tree lizards can be just as feisty as big iguanas. They hunt insects in low trees and bushes and they guard those territories like iguanas do. They have colorful dewlaps in yellow, orange, or bright red. Their dewlaps are big enough to be seen several feet away through the leaves. An anole displays its dewlap by spreading it out like a fan.

There are many species of anoles. They are all slim lizards with skinny heads and pointed snouts. Often they are different shades of green and brown. When they feel under attack their colors get darker. The Jamaican giant anole looks a bit like a green iguana because it has a row of spiky scales down its back and tail. It can grow to be twelve inches long, or even longer. That is very big for an anole.

On a car ride through Texas you might stop for a roadside rest. There you might see another iguanian crawling on the

WORDS to KNOW

ARBOREAL: *Arbor* means "tree." Arboreal animals spend most of their time living in trees. Many snakes and lizards are arboreal. But if you discover an arboreal turtle or alligator, please call a herpetologist right away!

Walk Like an Iguanian!

Lizards do not run like you or a dog. Can you run like a lizard? Start with your hands and knees on the ground. Put your arms in push-up position. Then make your legs do the splits and bend your knees. Ready to run? GO!

rocks. The collared lizard is about a foot or more in length. It is named after the two black rings on its neck, which look like a shirt collar. It's usually dressed with white spots and faint brown stripes across its body, but it turns brilliant colors during breeding season. If it feels trapped by you, it is likely to give you an angry bite. You would be better off to give it room to run—then you might see it zoom off on its two back legs!

For lizards with an even better two-legged trick, go all the way to Central America. There between North and South America is Costa Rica. Basilisks live in the forests of Costa Rica. If you stroll along a stream and scare a green basilisk, it may run right across the water and escape on the other side. The basilisk keeps its balance with its tail and some decorations that look like sails in the middle of its head, back, and tail. Because of its frilled feet and fast legs, it crosses the water without sinking. For this trick some people call the basilisks Jesus lizards.

In Australia there lives another iguanian that can outdo any anole's dewlap. It is the frilled lizard. When it feels threatened by a visitor, it will first open its mouth and hiss like a snake. Since its mouth is bright yellow inside, that is a bit scary. The small lizard also stands tall and spreads frills of skin all the way around its head. The frilled lizard is another lizard that tries to look bigger than it really is, but it is all an act. If its display doesn't make a big visitor leave, the frilled lizard will quickly run away.

FUN FACT

No Flapping Bat Wings, Just Batman Capes

Dracos are little flying dragons. There are forty-two species of them. Dracos have ribs that grow out of their chests into frills on both sides of their bodies. They spread their ribs to open the frills like a cape and sail from branch to branch in the rain forests of Thailand and Indonesia.

Prickly Little Iguanians

America's horned lizards and Australia's thorny devil (also called a thorny dragon) are alike for three reasons. First, both are desert lizards. Second, both search for anthills and gobble up ants by the hundreds. Third, these round little lizards are covered with scaly thorns. Cute and prickly!

Herpetologists have learned something amazing about the spikes on the thorny devil's back: They collect water. Here is how they work. You may notice some mornings that your shoes get soggy from the dew that collected on the grass overnight. The desert does not supply a thorny devil with much grass, so a thorny devil collects dew on its spikes. Then that water drips down its spikes, along ridges in its scales, and straight down to its mouth. Wow! Those little devils get a morning drink without moving a muscle!

Freaky Chameleons

Long ago ancient Greeks saw some wide-mouthed lizards. The Greeks expected them to roar. They thought each lizard looked like a "ground lion," and that is what *chameleon* means. That seems strange. Chameleons are not very big. They are super-fit for life in the trees, so they do not feel safe walking on the ground. You might think they look more like monkeys from outer space. Whatever you call them, they must be the weirdest lizards in the world.

There are over 150 species of chameleons. Like other iguanians, many have some decorations that do make them look fierce. They climb tall trees like iguanas, and they eat insects like anoles, but they do both in their weird way.

First, chameleons can climb or hang on very skinny branches. They can do this because the feet at the end of their long skinny legs are like clamps. Each foot has five toes like a normal lizard, but the toes are bunched into two groups (two in one bunch and three in the other). Those feet can grasp thin branches tightly. Most chameleons also have a tail that can grasp branches and support their bodies. A chameleon's shape also helps it walk steadily on thin branches because its body is narrow and flat on both sides. It does not have a wide belly like an iguana.

A chameleon's tongue is a super weapon for catching bugs. It is much longer than its body. As quick as a wink, a chameleon can launch it out of its mouth, grab a butterfly with it, and pull it back in. The tongue is sticky at the tip and has muscles for grabbing.

WORDS to KNOW

PREHENSILE: *Prehensile* means "for grasping and holding." A chameleon's prehensile tail grasps branches while its prehensile tongue grasps prey. An elephant's trunk is also prehensile.

Other lizards may change colors, but none can do the wonderful changes that chameleons can do. They can change slowly or quickly in response to their surroundings, their moods, or the sight of another chameleon. A chameleon makes itself look like a whole new lizard with a totally new pattern of color. They can pull out all the paints with red, lime, yellow, blue, black, pink, or more.

Weirder still are a chameleon's eyes. They are like two separate spy cameras. The left eye can look up while the right eye can look down. That way a chameleon can keep an eye on a grasshopper while looking out for a predator at the same time. With all these funny features, chameleons can make you laugh. Most chameleons live in Africa, including some of the funniest.

Africa's Funniest Chameleons

1. The dwarf chameleon (also called the minute leaf chameleon) is one of the world's smallest chameleons (about one inch). It still zaps teeny flies on the ground, but it must beware of large insects that could eat it!
2. The Parson's chameleon is the world's biggest chameleon (as long as twenty-six inches). The males have strange lumpy scales at the end of their nose.
3. The Jackson's chameleon makes some people say, "Look, a little triceratops!" Males have three horns on their heads that they use for fighting with each other.
4. The tiger chameleon is very skinny. Its chin sticks out from its frowning face. When it gets both eyes to look together at a bug, it looks like an old man.
5. The Namaqua desert chameleon has a look on its face that seems to say, "What am I doing here?" It is rare for a chameleon to live with almost no trees.

King Snake got all dressed up for Frilled Lizard's fancy party. Unfortunately, he arrived an hour late. What was his excuse?

Answer: "Sorry, Liz—on the way over here my tie kept sliding off!"

Skinks and Geckos

Nine hundred gecko species and more than 1,200 skink species make the biggest part of the lizard crowd. They are quite different than the iguanians. They do no head bobbing and have no frills or flaps. They have their own cool features.

Little Skinkers

You would think that with so many skinks in North America, more people would know what a skink is. The reason may be that these lowly lizards are hard to find! Most skinks live on or in the ground. They move fast and hide well. Most chase the prey they eat. That is very not iguanian! Chameleons never chase insects and iguanas never chase leaves!

Most skinks are smooth and sleek. Many have shiny scales that overlap. They have pointy snouts and pointy tails. Many skinks have rather small legs, and some have none at all. Skinks can also do another great lizard escape trick with their tails.

One skink species common throughout the eastern half of the United States is the five-lined skink. With its slender body lined in thin pale stripes, it looks like a prairie garter snake with legs! The long tail on an adult five-lined skink is gray, but a young five-lined skink has a bright blue tail.

Herpetologists think the blue tail is meant to fool a predator, such as a skunk. The skink would rather take a bite to its tail than its body. If a skunk does bite a skink's tail, the tail will break off. The skunk will have a tail left wiggling in its mouth while the skink runs away. Most skinks, geckos, and anoles can remove a tail to escape a predator. Lizards that do this can grow a new tail but not a perfect one.

The deserts of North Africa are home to a bizarre little skink. It is commonly called the sandfish. It may look like a fish out of water, but it is a lizard perfectly designed for an ocean of sand. The sandfish has a great scientific name, *Scincus scincus*. A sandfish has tiny legs. It is small enough to hold in your hand, where it will wiggle like crazy, and when you let it go it will dive and disappear below the sand before you can say "Hocus pocus, Scincus scincus."

There is a giant skink. Two feet long is giant for a skink. It is also called the Solomon Islands skink, since it lives on the Solomon Islands north of Australia. It lives very differently from most skinks. First, it lives in trees. Second, it has a prehensile tail like a chameleon or a possum. Third, it eats leaves.

What did the giant skink say as she slowly climbed up the big, big tree?

Answer: I skink I can. I skink I can! I skink I can!!

GET A GECKO!

Gerry and her sisters all got new pet geckos. They are deciding what to call them based on a set of rules. Can you figure out which name each girl would choose?

Gerry likes Gary but not Glenn
Gerry likes Tony but not Allen
Gerry likes Byron but not Simon
Which gecko name does Gerry like?
a. William b. Fred c. Andy d. Peter

Alma likes Steven but not Walter
Alma likes Robert but not Ken
Alma likes Norman but not Alex
Which gecko name does Alma like?
a. Nicholas b. Pedro c. Miki d. Allen

June likes Darren but not Rodrigo
June likes Johnny but not Yuki
June likes Kevin but not Stewart
Which gecko name does June like?
a. Wilbur
b. Bruce
c. Craig
d. Colin

CAN'T CATCH ME!

Not only do geckos shed their tail if caught but the tail continues to twitch, distracting the hunter as the gecko runs away.

Gecko, the Lizard That Says Its Name

The little geckos have froglike faces. Frogs make loud calling sounds, and so do geckos, but the geckos' are not as loud. Many geckos have been named after the calls they make. You may know Pikachu in Pokémon videos who runs around just saying "Pi-ka-chu!" Likewise, some geckos say "Geh-cko!" The fourteen-inch tokay geckos say "To-kay!" The little house geckos known as chi-chak geckos say "Chi-chak!"

In America families are used to squirrels living near the house. But in some warm Asian countries like Thailand, a family can become used to seeing a gecko in the house, on the wall, on the window pane, or on the ceiling. So can Texans and other people who live in the American South— lizards and other creatures get inside the house the way flies and spiders do.

Both geckos and anoles have sticky feet, but gecko feet stick better. Geckos climb better than Spider-Man! Here's how. Their feet do not have suction cups—that would not work on the rough trees that geckos climb. Their feet are not sticky like glue—that would make dirt and leaves stick to their feet. Geckos do have ridges on their feet, and on those ridges are hairs you can see only with a microscope. Those teeny-tiny hairs stick to all the teeny-tiny bumps on surfaces that look smooth to you, including the window. Gecko feet stick so well that the critters sort of have to peel their feet off some surfaces as they walk.

Monsters and Monitors

You can't learn about every lizard in one book, but you must learn about the poisonous ones and the dangerous ones.

Gila Monster and Beaded Lizard

Among the thousands of species of lizards, only two of them are poisonous. They are the American Gila monster and the Mexican beaded lizard. Both are desert lizards. The Gila monster is the smaller species, growing to between one and two feet long. The Mexican beaded lizard is bigger. It can grow to more than three feet long. They look similar. Both appear

WORDS to KNOW

AUTOTOMY: Some lizards drop off their tails to escape predators. This is called an *autotomy*, or the spontaneous casting off of a body part.

FUN FACT

Clean Your Eyes

Just like snakes, geckos have see-through eye caps instead of eyelids. Eye caps keep their eyes clean, just like your eyelids keep your eyes clean.

fierce and silly at the same time. They have wide mouths and very forked tongues. When they have eaten well, they are chubby lizards. They are covered in black, red, pink, or yellow scales that look like beads. These beads are called *osteoderms*, because they have bone (*oste-*) inside them. The bright osteoderms make their skin very strong. These details together make them look like fat cobs of colorful corn.

Gilas and beaded lizards eat mice, small rats, and small birds. They kill them with their venom, but the eggs they often eat do not need to be poisoned. Like many lizards, they store fat in their tails to live off of between meals. Gilas and beaded lizards have plenty of fat storage space in their tails and they need it when food is hard to find in the desert.

These lizards poison their prey differently than front-fanged snakes. They have venom that soaks up into their prey from the bottom of their jaws, not the top. While they chomp down on prey with a bite that is hard to open, the venom does its work on the prey. The bite and the venom of these lizards are very dangerous to humans, so people who live near them must practice safety.

KOMODO COUPLE

Komodo dragons are rated as "vulnerable" by scientists. This means their survival is endangered and they need protection. Here are some twins living in the safety of a zoo. Or are they twins? Can you spot the 7 differences?

Giant Lizards

Monitors include more lizard species with very forked tongues. They are strong, lean lizards. Most monitor species live in Australia. However, the most famous monitors live north of Australia. They are the Komodo dragons and they are the world's largest lizards.

Meeting them would take you to some volcanic islands again—this time Komodo island and its neighboring islands. This is where Komodo dragons grow to over six feet long and weigh up to 200 pounds. A Komodo has a big strong tail, a narrow head, a thick neck, and a belly that hangs when it walks. A Komodo sways its head to look around often, because its eyes do not move. It also has a mouth that opens very wide.

Komodos are not poisonous like Gila monsters, but their mouths are full of deadly bacteria. A deer or goat bitten by a Komodo may get away, but it will likely die from the nasty wound. Then the Komodo is sure to find it and feed on it and so will many others. Komodos hunt large animals without chasing them. Komodos also scavenge for dead animals to eat.

When Komodos feed on animals, they rip, tear, and swallow. Many mammal predators leave behind the bones of their prey. However, many reptiles eat and leave behind no bones. Reptiles have strong stomach acids that digest bones.

A Tuatara Is Not a Lizard

Finally, one more island visit, this time to some of New Zealand's tiny islands east of Australia. If you search the tiny islands, you will find what appears to be a dull lizard. However this twenty-two-inch scaly creature is different than a lizard. The original people of New Zealand called it the tuatara. This little reptile can live to be over 100 years old. It does not become full grown until it is thirty-five. You wouldn't want to wait that long to be big. Would you?

Be a Lizard Protector

You have learned about the many variations that lizards have in their same basic shape. Four legs and a tail can look

SAVE THE SNAKES!

Tuataras have been around since the time of the dinosaurs, but because of global warming they may soon be extinct. There are ways you can save snakes and lizards (and tuataras!). Ask your parents how to save energy around the house. Or start your own club. Put together these words to make names for your new club. We've started you off with one.

TORTOISE SARAH'S SAVERS
PETE'S LARRY'S GARY'S
LIZARD TINA'S LOUNGE PET
ROSIE'S REPTILE PALACE CRITTER
GANG REFUGE CAROL'S
SCALY TRAILER GREEN CLUB

SALLY'S SNAKE SANCTUARY

very different and be used very differently among lizards. Tongues and decorations on a lizard are also important to lizard survival for several reasons. You have also learned that one group of lizards has a lot in common with iguanas. Maybe you also noticed some clues in the last lizards you read about: very forked tongues, eyes that do not move, and mouths that open very wide, plus some of them were poisonous. Those are clues that lead herpetologists to believe that Gila monsters and monitors are the lizards most closely related to snakes.

Help Protect the Diversity of Lizards

Diversity means a collection of differences. Some of the world's most unusual lizards are rare and at risk of disappearing. There are things that can be done to protect lizard diversity in the wild. Here is one.

Don't Buy a Hot Lizard

Ask your local pet store how it gets its lizards, snakes, and turtles. Ask for proof. Every year many young reptiles or eggs are taken from the wild, brought into the United States illegally, and sold in stores. That is smuggling and it is a bad business that hurts the diversity of wild reptiles.

Last, remember that pet reptiles are creatures to care for, not things to collect. Let zoos collect animals.

SCIENTIFIC NAMES FOR LIZARDS

COMMON NAME	SCIENTIFIC NAME
WESTERN SLENDER GLASS LIZARD	*OPHISAURUS ATTENUATUS*
GALAPAGOS LAND IGUANA	*CONOLOPHUS SUBCRISTATUS*
COLLARED LIZARD	*CROTAPHYTUS COLLARIS*
GREEN BASILISK	*BASILISCUS PLUMIFRONS*
FRILLED LIZARD	*CHLAMYDOSAURUS KINGII*
MINUTE LEAF CHAMELEON	*BROOKESIA MINIMA*
FIVE-LINED SKINK	*EUMECES FASCIATUS*

Chapter 4
Turtles, Tortoises, Terrapins, Oh My!

Turtles can live in fresh water, on land, or in the ocean. A terrapin is what some people call a freshwater turtle. Tortoises normally live on dry land. You might call them all turtles, but you can also use the name that herpetologists have for the turtle group, the *Testudines*. The number of Testudine species is not as great as the snake and lizard species in the *Squamata* group. In fact, the number of turtle species is far lower than the number of snake species alone. However, the shape and anatomy of turtles are just as amazing as snakes' are.

Shelter Built Into the Backbone

Turtles have an unmistakable shape all their own. While some folks might mistake a salamander for a lizard or assume a legless lizard is a snake, everyone can recognize a turtle's unique body and shell. However, not everyone understands how a turtle is built. Maybe on TV you have seen a cartoon turtle step out of its shell wearing polka-dot shorts. Real turtles never suffer such embarrassment because they cannot leave their shells.

The Shell Is Part of the Turtle

Remember the words *endoskeleton* and *exoskeleton*? A turtle has both. It has an endoskeleton to help its body stand and move, and it has an exoskeleton to protect it from predators. A turtle's shell is its exoskeleton. It acts like the protective skull bone you have around your brain. So a turtle also has bone around its body. Use your imagination again and picture what you would be as a turtle.

Zookeeper Ned ordered Zookeeper Ed to fetch a Brazilian turtle from South America. Months later a slow rumble roused Ned from his office. Ned saw Ed shepherding a herd of turtles through the gate! Ed said to Ned, "I know you wanted a lot, but I don't think I got a BRAZILLION turtles."

If you were a turtle, first you would grow a tail made out of vertebrae extended past your rear legs. As a turtle you would likely have a short tail; your wide sturdy body would not need a long tail for balance like a lizard's. If you were a turtle, your ribs would grow connected to both sides of your backbone to make a large rib cage. Your turtle rib cage would be very different because your shoulder and hip bones would be inside your rib cage! The bones that together make your shell would be permanently bonded to your backbone and ribs. So as a turtle you'd be "out of your mind" to try getting out of your shell!

The Key to Turtle Survival

The top part of a turtle shell is called the *carapace*. The bottom part beneath a turtle's belly is the *plastron*; it is connected to the carapace by what is called the *bridge*. Turtle shells can be very beautiful.

Other animals have shells but none are the same as a turtle shell. For example, lobsters and crabs have shells but they outgrow their shells like you outgrow your clothes. A turtle does not outgrow its shell. A turtle and its shell grow bigger together. A snail shell also grows, but a snail shell is not made of bone and skin. Some turtles have soft leathery skin over their shell bones, but most have tough scaly skin. That means a turtle can feel you touch its carapace!

The large scales on turtle shells are called *scutes*. The scutes on the edge of a turtle's carapace are usually small and the scutes in the middle of the carapace are usually big. These large scales sometimes look like square or pentagon shapes. The scutes on turtle shells can be very plain or full of patterns. Some turtle shells look like wonderful painted pottery or creative sculptures.

For example, the carapace of an Indian starred tortoise has about ten raised peaks that look like small mountains on its back. It also has bold stripes on each scute. Another curious

FUN FACT

Breathing in a Tight Suit of Armor

As they breathe, turtles cannot move their chests like you do. So they have developed some different ways to get oxygen. Some turtles get air by using the muscles of their legs to pump air into their lungs as they walk.

TryThis

Discover the Average Scute Number

Herpetologists record lots of information. Try recording some for yourself. Examine five turtles at the pet store or zoo. Record how many scutes were on each turtle's carapace. Draw five big circles, one for each turtle. Arrange pennies inside each circle to represent each turtle's scutes. Rearrange the pennies to make all the turtles the same, or "average." Leftover pennies might happen.

FUN FACT

Turtles Are Older Than the Dinosaurs

You won't find turtles that old alive, but if you own a turtle you can say its ancestors lived before the T. rex. Your turtle's prehistoric ancestors aren't its grandparents; they are its great, great, great . . . (KEEP GOING; you'd have to say "great" for a VERY LONG time to describe your turtle's prehistoric ancestors) grandparents.

carapace belongs to the yellow-blotched map turtle of southern Mississippi. With rounded spikes down the middle and bright yellow spots on each scute, this turtle sometimes looks like an alien emerging from a very strange flying saucer.

Having a shell has helped turtles survive on Earth for more than 200 million years. In many ways turtles have stayed the same for a very long time. However, many different turtles have adapted to a variety of habitats. In the next sections you will meet more handsome turtles that show how they have adapted their shells, necks, legs, feet, and claws to survival in different habitats. You will also learn the turtle ways of moving and eating.

Strollers on Land

A very good example of a common tortoise is the Russian tortoise. Strangely, however, Russian tortoises are less common in Russia than in some Asian countries that end with "an," like Iran, Uzbekistan, and Afghanistan. These rugged reptiles live in dry lands with sparse plants and weather that gets very hot and very cold. A Russian tortoise is normally about eight to ten inches long. Like many tortoises it has a dome-shaped carapace, like a large hard hamburger bun. Its legs have tough protective scales, and its feet have pointy claws. To hide from a predator the Russian tortoise pulls its head and legs into its shell and covers its head with its well-armored front legs.

Back to the Galapagos Islands

To meet some rare and remarkable tortoises, you can take another imaginary journey back to the Galapagos Islands. The world's largest tortoises live there. Male Galapagos tortoises can weigh more than 500 pounds and have carapaces more than four feet long. Their legs are strong pillars with dull round claws. Their legs look like small scaly elephant legs.

TASTY TORTOISE TIDBITS

Tortoises live in dry areas where food is often hard to find. Can you unscramble the letters to see what kind of things this tortoise might eat? To find what they should NOT eat, read the shaded letters.

SEDEW = _ _ _ _

NROC = _ _ _ _

SARSG = _ _ _ _ _

NNILADEOD = _ _ _ _ _ _ _ _ _

SHREB = _ _ _ _ _

STACUC = _ _ _ _ _ _

MILCUAM = _ _ _ _ _ _ _

TREWA = _ _ _ _ _

SWEFLOR = _ _ _ _ _ _ _

ROLVEC = _ _ _ _ _ _

HORYICC = _ _ _ _ _ _ _

DEVIEN = _ _ _ _ _ _

A HERD OF TURTLES IS CALLED A BALE.

TOOTHLESS TORTOISE

Tortoises have no teeth. But that's not a problem for them—they just use their horn-covered jaws to tear food into small enough pieces to swallow.

People travel across the world to visit these gentle giants. Size is not the only curious thing about them. The Galapagos tortoises are not all the same. They are different depending on which island they live. Long before people ever discovered them, these tortoises lived here. Those that survived grew well adapted to the islands. Some islands have different plants to eat. Some islands are warmer, some are cooler. Tortoises in cooler greener places have shorter necks for eating low grasses. Tortoises on warmer, dryer, less green islands have longer necks for eating tall prickly cactus plants. The carapaces of these long-neck tortoises are also shaped like a horse's saddle instead of a dome. The saddle shape allows these tortoises to reach their necks higher and keep their bodies cooler. Time in these special places has created different species of tortoise.

The Shell Is Not Really a House

When you were very young you may have been told that a turtle is an animal that "carries its house on its back." That is not really true. Some tortoises and other turtles still need a home like other scaly creatures. In fact, the gopher tortoise is a great home builder.

The gopher tortoise is not much longer than a foot. You might find one in Georgia or Florida. It builds tunnels. With claws designed for digging, it works on one tunnel or more all its life. Some gopher tortoise tunnels are thirty feet long. These tunnels make such good shelter that even some gophers prefer gopher tortoise tunnels over their own. Many other creatures use gopher tortoise tunnels as a place to stay. If you discover a gopher tortoise tunnel, be warned that a rattlesnake might have moved in too!

While you cannot call a turtle's shell its house, you may call it the turtle's emergency shelter or maybe its panic room. Box turtles have the best shells for emergencies. If a predator gets too close to a box turtle, the turtle can pull its head and all four legs into its shell. And it can close up its shell tightly until the predator goes away. That is something you may have seen a cartoon turtle do on TV. This time it's true!

Box turtles like those found in South or North Carolina or Virginia are not called tortoises, but they do live on land. Those eastern box turtles often have orange-yellow spots on their faces and carapaces. If you turn one over you can see the hinge on its plastron. The hinge allows a box turtle to close up its shell.

Divers in Fresh Water

Most turtle species are freshwater turtles. They are similar to many snakes and some iguanas that find food or safety near or in rivers, streams, lakes, or ponds. Freshwater turtles have adapted themselves to spend even more time in the water. Freshwater turtles are excellent swimmers. They have their own ways of hunting for food in and around the water.

Some freshwater turtles eat only meat. Many, however, eat both plants and animals, including dead creatures they find. That makes freshwater turtles excellent omnivores.

Timid but Tough Turtles

In North America the painted turtle may be the most common freshwater turtle. Although it can be found in many places, a close look at one is not easy to get. A painted turtle near or in a pond will quickly disappear into the water when threatened. So only very lucky or very quiet turtle watchers may closely spy on a wild painted turtle.

Touching one proves that its shell is hard and smooth. To help it swim, a painted turtle's shell is also shaped like a shallow cereal bowl instead of the helmet shape that a common tortoise has. Its carapace is dark brownish green but the edge is painted with patches of red. Its head has yellow stripes. Its legs and neck may have stripes of yellow and red, but its greatest colors can be seen underneath on its plastron. A full-grown painted turtle shell is about six inches long. Painted turtles have long claws on their feet for digging the ground, tearing food, and climbing logs.

WORDS to KNOW

CARRION: *Carrion* means dead or rotten animal meat. Some snakes, many freshwater turtles, and certainly Komodo dragons think that finding a piece of carrion is a tasty discovery. Yuck!

PERFECT POT

While having a pet turtle can be fun, consider saving them in their natural habitat. Just like us, they prefer their own homes. This turtle is trying to decide which is the perfect clay pot to move into. He's decided it must have **1.** One stripe **2.** Two flowers **3.** No cracks and **4.** Two handles.

KEEP THEM WILD: The best way to help turtles is not to buy them at the pet store. If you buy them, the store will have to get more and this further reduces the numbers living in the wild.

The stare of a painted turtle shows its round pupils. Those are your clue that a painted turtle is *diurnal*, meaning that it is a daytime hunter. In its weedy, muddy habitat it gobbles plants and small water creatures like tadpoles, insects, and snails.

Other turtles, called mud turtles, are often an inch or two smaller than a painted turtle and are much less colorful. Their name tells you they are the color of mud. There are several species of mud turtles.

Mud and painted turtles both have what all freshwater turtles need for swimming: webbed feet that work like flippers. You would have webbed feet too if you had thin skin stretched between your toes.

Something else special about a turtle is its mouth. Turtles do not have teeth. Instead, a turtle has a hard edge on the top and on the bottom of its mouth. Those two hard edges are made of the same tough keratin that is in all reptile scales. Some turtles have sharp-edged mouths and others have flat-edged mouths, depending on whether they tear or crush their food. With hard mouths and strong jaws, some turtles can give a bite like a pinch from sharp pliers that will not let go!

Monster Turtle

Imagine you just climbed a tree. Below you lies a pond, a meadow of tall grass, and a sandy hill. You hear a splash. First you see the grass rustling and falling down but you do not see anyone there. Still, something is making a path toward the hill. Then from the grass and onto the sand comes a monstrous turtle. It is a mother "snapper" about to lay her eggs in the sandy hill.

This snapping turtle's carapace is commonly a foot and a half long. It is named for its sharp mouth. If you were to climb down from your tree for a closer look, you would need to leave some space between you and the mother snapper. Although this turtle would avoid you in the water, it will bite creatures that come close to it on land. A common snapping turtle can bite off a person's finger.

Common snappers like that one are tough North American turtles. They wear their small carapaces like a

FUN FACT

Pretty Good Climbers!

Some species of mud turtle are quite good at climbing up trees that lean near water, but they are NOT arboreal turtles. They are still freshwater turtles.

FUN FACT

Two Turtle Groups

Herpetologists try to divide turtles into two groups depending on how they hide their heads. Most pull their heads backward into their shells. But some in Australia and South America fold and tuck their necks to the side. So which group gets China's big-headed turtle? Its head is too big to hide either way.

muscle man in a small shirt. This means their shells are not big enough to hide their large legs. For that reason their legs have tough scales like armor, as tortoise legs do. Snappers also cannot hide their large heads behind their front legs. That is why they will protect themselves with a bite.

They are big eaters. Food for them is mostly animals of many kinds. They will eat amphibians and fish. They will even eat small birds and mammals that enter their waters.

The common snapping turtle is not the largest freshwater turtle in North America. The largest is the alligator snapping turtle. It can weigh more than 200 pounds. It is also a living example of how turtles may have looked millions of years ago. Parts of its body look as herpetologists believe prehistoric turtles did, including a long tail and a jagged edge around its carapace. The bumpy top of its carapace looks like an alligator's back. Its hard mouth looks like a parrot's beak. Its neck appears to wear a spiked dog collar, but it is actually covered with soft pointy scales. It is the monster turtle.

An alligator snapper can eat what the common snappers do, plus more. It will even eat small turtles. It also gets food in a way no other turtles can. It goes fishing at the bottom of a river with its own bait. It sits with its mouth wide open at the river bottom. The only part of its body it moves is the red wiggling end of its tongue. That looks like a worm. Fish that try to take the bait get the big bite.

Would You Like Hard Shell or Soft Shell?

In North America, Asia, and Africa you have a choice. On those three continents freshwater turtles have either shells covered with hard scutes or shells covered with soft leathery skin.

The spiny softshell turtle is one that has developed a shell without scutes. Instead it has a carapace like a big floppy pancake. In the middle of that pancake you may see the bumps of its vertebrae down the middle of its back just like yours, except that these turtle vertebrae are still connected to a shell. In fact, if you touched the spiny softshell you could feel that it does indeed have a shell bone beneath the skin, but touching the spiny softshell would not be safe. Warning: it has a very long neck. It can easily reach its head around and give you a sharp bite

Spiny softshell turtles live across half of the United States including the central, eastern, and southern states. Most have spiny points on the edge of the carapace near their heads. All have skinny stretched-out pig noses. Such a nose can peek out of a lake to breathe while the turtle stays under water. Spiny softshells have bright stripes behind their eyes and dark polka dots on their backs.

Softshell turtles can stay under water for a long time because they can also get oxygen through their skin like amphibians. While a softshell turtle searches for food at the bottom of a pond, the skin on its long neck and its flat shell can absorb extra oxygen. This allows a spiny softshell turtle enough oxygen reserves to bury itself at the bottom of a pond and wait for a crayfish to swim close and become its next meal.

Cruisers in the Ocean

Seven species of turtle live as no other turtles can. They live in the ocean. Other than sea snakes, perhaps no other reptiles than the sea turtles are so well adapted to eating, swimming, and sleeping in the sea. Besides being marine reptiles, sea turtles are also remarkable for their great size. Here they are listed in order from smallest to largest.

Seven Species of Sea Turtles
1. Olive ridley sea turtles have similar size and appearance as the Kemp's ridleys.
2. Kemp's ridley sea turtles live only in or near the Gulf of Mexico.
3. Hawksbill sea turtles have an upper jaw that looks like a hawk's bill.
4. Flatback sea turtles live in waters near Australia.
5. Loggerhead sea turtles are bigger than alligator snapping turtles.
6. Green sea turtles eat green algae and seagrass.
7. Leatherback sea turtles can weigh as much as 2,000 pounds!

GLUB GLUB!

How long can you hold your breath? Definitely not as long as this super turtle! Read the numbered boxes to find out if you could match his time.

9 life	20 for	4 turtle
14 It	17 its	21 five
3 sea	15 can	13 ocean
19 underwater	11 the	26 while
7 of	1 The	29 and
12 deep	23 at	10 in
28 seagrass	5 spends	27 eating
16 hold	22 hours	30 algae.
25 time	18 breath	6 most
2 green	8 its	24 a

Turtles Built for Speed!

All sea turtles have a carapace shaped for smooth swimming. It is smaller and less heavy. It is wide in the front and narrow in the back. Sea turtles cannot hide their heads and legs inside their shells. Instead of clawed or webbed feet they have flippers. They spread their front legs like wings while their rear legs steer like rudders at the back of a boat. This all helps sea turtles swim at speeds greater than twenty miles per hour. No tortoise can walk that fast!

Life in the Great Wide Ocean

If you are lucky enough to see a sea turtle on a beach, you might notice tears in its eyes. Those tears are another way that sea turtles have adapted to life in the ocean. A sea turtle must get rid of the ocean's salt that collects in its body, so it cries out the salt. Do you remember the marine iguanas that sneeze out ocean salt?

While some freshwater turtles may live their whole lives in and around one small pond, many sea turtles swim thousands of miles across the ocean. These long travels they make are called *migrations*. Sea turtles migrate farther than any other reptile.

Now that you have learned that turtles are not as simple as some people may think, you may want to help protect the slow tortoises of the land, the freshwater turtles of the wetlands, and the mighty turtles of the sea.

Be a Buddy to the Turtles

If you want to be a buddy to turtles, then help protect their habitats. Keep them clean. For example, if you walk or play near the ocean, please help keep garbage off the beach. Junk like plastic bags can drift far across the ocean and hurt a sea turtle that eats it by mistake.

Eutrophication is another example of pollution that is bad for turtles, but it is not another kind of garbage. Instead eutrophication means overfeeding a pond, lake, or small slow stream. You would not want to overfeed an animal like your pet; likewise overfeeding a freshwater habitat is harmful to the creatures inside. For example, people feed the grass in their front lawns with fertilizers. If rain washes that plant food into a nearby pond, that food feeds tiny floating algae. Algae are like plants but not the same, because they use up the same oxygen that turtles and other creatures breathe in a pond. This is how eutrophication chokes a pond.

More Advice for a Young Herpetologist Outdoors

If you want to tell people how important the protection of local reptile habitats is, then exploring those habitats is your first step. Besides, visiting turtle territories is fun! So along with boots, a walking stick, and a responsible friend, consider bringing along a few other things to make your turtle hiking more interesting.

TURTLE TRADITIONS

Turtles have figured large in history. According to ancient Hindu tradition, a turtle carried the elephants that supported the earth on their backs.

There are some famous modern turtles too. Can you make out who these are by unscrambling the letters?

EETYRL HET RETTUL

NEEGATE TUNTAM JAINN ULTERST

POAKO

Here is a list of things you might want to have handy on your next hike.

Turtle Hike Checklist

1. Small pair of binoculars—for when you want a closer look at a turtle
2. Digital camera—a cool tool to start a reptile photo collection
3. Notebook—for drawings and records of observations of reptiles you see
4. Felt-tip pens—much more dependable than a pencil or a ballpoint pen outside
5. Field guide book—a quick reference to help you identify species you see
6. Bottle of water—for thirst on a long hike

Please Keep Wild Reptiles in the Wild

If you find a turtle while out on a hike and you somehow catch it, please do not take it home as a pet. Your state's Department of Natural Resources requires people to buy a license to keep a wild turtle. Rules like that are meant to protect wild reptiles. If you want a pet turtle, buy one that was laid and hatched in captivity.

SCIENTIFIC NAMES FOR TURTLES

COMMON NAME	SCIENTIFIC NAME
RUSSIAN TORTOISE	*TESTUDO HORSFIELDII*
GOPHER TORTOISE	*GOPHERUS POLYPHEMUS*
PAINTED TURTLE	*CHRYSEMYS PICTA*
SPINY SOFTSHELL	*APALONE SPINIFERUS*

Chapter 5

The Kings of the Reptiles

Near a South Carolina lake shore, a small reptile sits with its four feet and its long tail perched on top of what could be a floating log. The scaly creature is only ten inches long. It has large eyes with skinny pupils like a gecko. Strangely, it does not dive into the water as a shy turtle would do when it sees you approach. It seems to smile like a garter snake. Does it know something that you don't? It does. It knows that it is not sitting on a log. It is sitting on its mother, an eight-foot American alligator. In about six years this baby alligator may grow to the same size as its mother. It will grow to be a king of the reptiles.

American alligators belong to the last group of reptiles for you to learn. They are one of the twenty-three mighty crocodilians. That is very few compared to the many different species of lizards, snakes, and even turtles. The crocodilians are mighty because of their great size, strong jaws, tough scales, and fierce hunting. Alligators and crocodiles are not the only crocodilians. Alligators include the very similar caimans. The unusual-looking gharial of Asia is a unique crocodile compared to both the alligators and the crocodiles. Whether big or small, crocodilians are living armored all-terrain vehicles built to move well on land and in water. Read on and learn how they are built, how they move, and how they hunt.

Chameleon bragged to Alligator, "Look. I can change colors. Bet you can't."

"Wow, you really camouflaged yourself," said Alligator. "I bet you could even become invisible."

"Really! How?" said Chameleon.

"Like this," replied Alligator. Chomp!

I'm Croc, and I'm a Crocodilian!

The largest reptile in North America is the American crocodile, yet many people in the United States have never seen one. Much of its habitat is in Central and South America near the coasts of the Atlantic and Pacific Oceans. Very southern Florida is the only place in the United States where American crocodiles live. Crocodiles or "crocs" live in both fresh water and salt water, and in southern Florida both mingle in the Everglades. The Everglades is a large area of swampland with shallow waters, saw grass, and mangrove trees.

A Big Bite

The world has fourteen species of crocodiles. The American crocodile is one of the biggest. American crocodiles usually grow to about fifteen feet long, but American crocs in the Everglades are smaller than those found outside of the United States.

American crocs dine mostly on fish but they also crunch crabs and turtles. For an American croc to break a tough turtle shell, it needs strong jaws. All crocodilians are armed with great jaw muscles for closing their mouths. They have less muscle for opening their mouths, which allows brave and strong herpetologists to hold their mouths shut when handling them.

Crocodilian teeth are made to pierce and hold prey. A crocodilian's tooth is quickly replaced when it falls out. Each tooth is cone-shaped and hollow. Teeth in use are stacked like plastic cups on top of the replacement teeth below.

Asia also has crocs. India and Pakistan, for example, have a species commonly called a mugger. Besides living in calm waters of lakes and streams, mugger crocs seem to live well in watering holes created by people. Muggers will walk long distances to find better waters in which to feed.

Kid: I hate going to the dentist.
Croc: Really? I love dentists.
Kid: How often do you go?
Croc: I go through many dentists a year.
Kid: Did you say you go TO many dentists?
Croc: They stick their little heads in my mouth, and I must go through at least seven of them a year. Yes, I love dentists.

FUN FACT

Yucky Fish Bait

An American crocodile eats lots of fish. Sometimes it uses bait to catch them. Where does the croc get it? It throws up partially digested food. When a hungry fish approaches for a taste of the bait the croc will snap the fish up.

CROCODILE ROCKIN'

Crocodiles are another reptile that doesn't get fair treatment. They can definitely be dangerous, but they're just protecting themselves and their homes. It's best to steer clear of them and let them live their lives.

Here's a pond full of crocs having fun.
Two of them are twins—can you find them?

WHAT DO YOU DO IF YOU FIND A CROCODILE IN YOUR TOILET?

Fortunately, muggers, like most crocodilians, can walk better than lizards. Lizards are built to walk with their front and back legs sticking straight from their bodies, as your arms might when doing a push-up. A mugger croc can do a "high walk." It can lift its body well off the ground with its legs pressed near its body and walk with its feet underneath itself.

Ready to Submerge!

Africa is home to a famous species of croc. The Nile crocodile is named after the world's longest river. Nile crocodiles live along the Nile river and across central Africa.

When a crocodile slides into the muddy waters of the Nile it seals its body like a diving submarine. Its nostrils close to keep out water. Under its two outer eyelids it has a third see-through eyelid that closes across the eye and protects the eye while submerged. A muscular flap in the back of its throat closes tight so it can open its mouth without swallowing water. Also, its ears, unlike the noticeable open circles on lizards, close up so that they look like slits behind the eyes. All crocodilians have these watertight features.

An adult Nile crocodile's body is dark olive green and made to swim. All crocodilians are super swimmers. All crocodilians use their feet like paddles for quick underwater steering. Each foot has five toes with webbing in between. Crocodilians are narrow in the front, wide in the middle, and narrow at the end. This shape lets them gracefully slide through the water. They are powered by their strong tails. They move their tails in an S shape like snakes and iguanas do when they swim.

Smaller Nile crocs eat fish, reptiles, birds, amphibians, and small mammals. Large Nile crocs will eat larger mammals when they get the chance. A Nile croc's best way of killing large prey is to take it below the water and drown it.

Try This

Open Wide Like a Croc

Lie with your stomach and chin on the floor. Open your mouth a few times. Since you normally drop your jaw to open your mouth, lifting your head to say "ah" like a croc feels strange. However, like a croc you also use more muscles for closing your mouth than for opening it.

FuN FACT

Saltie's Special Tongue

Crocodiles cannot stick out their tongues, but they need them. Saltwater crocs absorb salt from ocean water but must get rid of it. It comes out in the saliva that oozes from glands in their tongues. So sea turtles cry out excess salt, marine iguanas sneeze it out, and salties drool it out.

Australia has the world's biggest species of crocodilian. It is the saltwater crocodile and Australians call it the saltie. No other crocodilian swims farther into the sea than the saltie. It will sometimes travel hundreds of miles into the Pacific. People also consider the saltie to be the most aggressive croc. Do not even think of swimming anywhere near these crocs. They can eat you!

I'm Gator, and I'm a Crocodilian!

If you watch alligators (gators for short) and you watch crocs, you will soon be able to recognize their differences. Gators have a wider U-shaped snout while crocs have a narrower V-shaped snout. Gators are also darker in color than crocodiles. Do not get close enough to experience these differences. An American alligator has even stronger jaws than the crocodiles, with over 2,000 pounds of pressure in its bite. Imagine a 2,000-pound hippo putting all its weight on your foot!

There are two species of gators in the world, the American alligator and Chinese alligator. The American gator grows to about thirteen feet and the Chinese gator grows to about six feet. The American gator shares habitat with the American croc in Florida and lives in several other southeastern states. The Chinese gator is found only in China's Yangtze River valley.

Both species are nocturnal, or nighttime hunters. The Chinese gator eats smaller prey such as snails, clams, and fish. The American gator eats larger prey. Ambush is its method of hunt. It waits motionless for animals to come to it.

Crocodilians are built so they can float right near the surface of the water unnoticed. Like anacondas, they have eyes and nostrils on the top of their head, so they can breathe and watch without revealing themselves.

Large crocodilians like the American gator are top predators. That means they eat at the top of the food chain.

Their hunting controls the numbers of animals in many species in their habitats.

I'm Caiman, and I'm a Crocodilian!

All six of the caiman species live in Central and South America. Some caiman species are small and look like young alligators. The black caiman, however, is large. It grows larger than the American alligator. The Cuvier's dwarf caiman has large eyes and a short snout. It is the smallest of the crocodilians. It normally grows to about four and half feet.

A small caiman is still tough. One reason why is the armor that they wear like all crocodilians. They are covered with tough osteoderms, bone-filled scales, larger than the beadlike ones on Gila monsters. A caiman's, gator's, or croc's back feels like leather stretched over rock. A crocodilian's belly, however, is much softer, but certainly not as soft as a frog's belly!

I'm Gharial, and I'm a Crocodilian!

India has the most bizarre-looking species of crocodilian. It is the gharial. It can grow to about twenty-one feet long. A full-grown male gharial looks a bit like a sausage covered in armor with large bug-eyes and a scissors for a mouth. The gharial also has a large bulb at the end of its snout.

The gharial's long skinny mouth might look strange but it is very useful for catching fish. Because of its shape a gharial can quickly move its head to snatch fish in rushing waters. A fish caught in a gharial's razor-sharp teeth is not likely to get free. Gharials have more teeth than any other crocodilian. Crocs normally have close to seventy teeth. Gators and caimans have around eighty teeth. Gharials have over a hundred teeth.

COME ON CAIMAN

Caimans are from South and Central America. Some pets were released into the wild in North America and now you can find them here! What does a caiman say when you ask how he got here?*

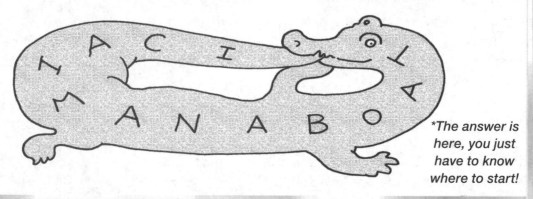

*The answer is here, you just have to know where to start!

Of all the crocodilians, the gharials may be best suited for water and least fit for land. They have short legs and cannot high walk. They crawl on their bellies. However they swim very well in fast-moving river waters. In fact, the gharial's scientific name, *Gavialis gangeticus,* includes the name of India's greatest river, the Ganges.

In the 1970s the gharials came close to joining the dinosaurs on the list of extinct animals. They have increased in numbers since then, but they are presently in danger and in small numbers again. One threat to gharials is fishing nets.

Be a Friend to Crocodilians . . . from a Distance!

Respect is one great thing that large predators like crocodilians can teach people. Looking at a smart scaly creature that is bigger than you is a powerful experience.

TOOTHY SMILE

The most noticeable feature of the gharial is the long narrow snout with a bulbous shape at the end. There's one more feature that makes the gharial unique. To find out what it is, cross out the letters that don't appear in the list below. The remaining letters spell out the answer.

A, D, E, H, N, O, R, T, U,

C	T	V	F	F	H	C	P	E	B
X	W	I	Y	M	H	G	I	J	K
A	B	B	C	P	Q	Z	V	Z	E
C	C	C	Z	I	L	L	M	G	I
B	U	F	F	P	K	K	T	M	O
J	J	K	B	C	X	Y	X	I	M
O	P	N	E	P	P	H	K	U	N
X	D	R	W	E	I	I	D	C	A
I	I	M	N	I	D	M	P	F	C
S	T	S	E	W	W	J	L	N	L
T	V	V	J	L	S	E	B	B	E
S	K	L	T	S	M	M	H	I	B

What words can you make using the letters in this word? We found 5, but there are more.

GHARIAL

Give Them Some Space

Respecting crocodilians is a safe thing to do. For example, feeding pigeons is okay. Feeding wild gators is not. Wild animals can grow very bold when you feed them frequently, whether they are squirrels or alligators. So if your part of the country is home to gators or you visit gator country, remember that wild alligators that receive free food this way lose their fear of humans and become more dangerous. Only observe gators and crocs in the wild from a great distance.

Another way people can respect the mighty crocodilians is to give them the space they need to live. They are large predators that need large habitats. Many crocodilians are considered endangered species because people now live in places where crocodilians once did.

Get Involved

If you enjoy all kinds of reptiles from little geckos to big gators, then consider joining a group of other people who are friendly to reptiles. Many states have such groups, which are called herpetological societies. Your town may have one! Members of most herpetological societies include people who work with reptiles, people who study them, and people young and old who are simply interested in them. They are people interested in preserving reptile habitats. A herpetological society meeting is a good place to learn what reptiles are endangered in your area. Some herpetological societies also find homes for reptile pets that have been improperly cared for, including alligators!

SCIENTIFIC NAMES FOR CROCODILIANS

COMMON NAME	SCIENTIFIC NAME
AMERICAN CROCODILE	CROCODYLUS ACUTUS
NILE CROCODILE	CROCODYLUS NILOTICUS
AMERICAN ALLIGATOR	ALLIGATOR MISSISSIPPIENSIS

Chapter 6
Amazing Reptilian Adaptations

A girl was in the bathroom with her herpetology book and crayons for hours until her mom opened the door and was shocked. On every square of the floor the girl had drawn a different picture of a scaly creature. The girl proudly said, "Now our bathroom has a rep-TILE floor!"

WORDS to KNOW

BIOLOGY: Biology means "life study." It's a science for studying living things: plants, animals, and tiny living things too small to see. Herpetology is a special kind of biology for studying reptiles and amphibians.

Y ou are smart, so you can learn quickly. When you learn to do something new, you *adapt*. Biology studies how species of animals can adapt too. For example, the Galapagos marine iguanas learned to eat food from the ocean. Sometimes a species can make a change or adaptation quickly. Other adaptations are made over a long time, especially changes in the anatomy of a species. For example, think of a rattlesnake. It is much like a fast car with unneeded parts removed to make it perform well. A mechanic calls such a car "stripped down." One way to understand rattlesnakes today is to think of their many ancestor reptiles over millions of years slowly stripped down to just the parts that helped them survive. Legs, arms, ears—rattlers don't need them! Instead, rattlers have incredible folding fangs. Those fangs were a slow change in rattlesnake anatomy.

Not Little Dinosaurs

If you want to better understand how reptiles developed some of their special adaptations, it helps to explore their history on the earth. Imagine the world long, long ago—before humans, before dinosaurs, before reptiles.

Amphibian Ancestors

Paleontologists piece together clues from the past to tell how life was before people. Fossils are some of their best clues. Here is how paleontologists believe reptiles got their start on Earth. During a long time called the *Paleozoic Era* more than 500 million years ago, the oceans were home to all creatures with backbones. For millions of years those vertebrates swam the seas while on land plants grew. Invertebrates, like insects, also began buzzing and wiggling on land. Amphibians were the first vertebrates to step on land and eat those creatures that buzzed and wiggled. Paleontologists believe that offspring of amphibians later developed features that helped them live better on dry land. They grew scaly skin and they laid eggs with shells that did not dry out. The Earth grew different kinds of reptiles. Among them would be the dinosaurs.

What Made Dinosaurs Different?

During the next long time called the *Mesozoic Era*, more and more land creatures developed. Reptiles grew great in number, size, and variety. That is why some paleontologists called that time the Age of Reptiles, although small mammals did scurry along the ground among the large reptiles. During the Mesozoic Era (about 230 million years ago), the earth also became home to the dinosaurs.

Paleontologists believe dinosaurs were like today's reptiles in some ways and different in others. Certainly all dinosaurs had scaly skin and strong bones like today's reptiles, but paleontologists are not sure if all dinosaurs were cold-blooded. Dinosaurs certainly did not creep like the reptiles you know. Today crocs, lizards, and turtles only sometimes do a "high walk" on their short legs, but dinosaurs had long strong legs. It was easy for them to stand high off the ground on four legs or on two. Many two-legged dinosaurs ran very much like chickens. Some dinosaurs even had feathers. In fact, some paleontologists suspect that dinosaurs are more closely related to birds than to snakes and lizards.

What does this mean for a young herpetologist like you? It means that today's reptiles are not little dinosaurs.

PALEONTOLOGIST: *Paleontologists* are special biologists who study prehistoric animals or plants. Some of them study dinosaurs.

FOSSILS: Fossils are body parts or prints left behind in the earth by animals that died long ago. Some fossils are just small pieces of bone. Other fossils found are whole skeletons with skin still attached. Digging for fossils takes careful, patient work.

Back to Class with Reptiles

The many turtles, the little tuataras, and the mighty crocodilians are very old sorts of reptiles. They have changed very little since the dinosaur days. Of the reptiles, you know that snakes may have been the last to develop on Earth. Today herpetologists also think about the prehistoric beginnings of reptile species when they classify them.

To *classify* means to put into groups, like sorting out laundry into piles of socks, shirts, and shorts. Students in school are usually grouped into classes according to their age. That is classification. When herpetologists classify the many different species of reptiles, they understand the reptiles better.

Classifying reptiles is not easy. Herpetologists often discuss different ways to group them. Here is one reason why. To make groups you need rules like "ALL these kids are twelve" or "NEVER put dirty socks over there." However, while herpetologists make rules, reptiles can break the rules since they are living creatures. The more you learn about them, the more you realize how hard it is to confidently say "ALL" or "NEVER" when you talk about reptiles.

Herpetologists use big words to give each reptile species a scientific name. That makes classification easier because the common names that people give to scaly creatures can be confusing. Look at these reptiles listed with their confusing common names like the milk shake—sorry, the milk snake!

Confusing Reptile Names
- *Lampropeltis triangulum*, a.k.a. milk snake, does not drink milk.
- *Elaphe guttata,* a.k.a. corn snake, does not eat corn. Corn snakes and milk snakes do, however, eat the rodents that eat corn meant to feed milk cows.
- *Micrurus fulvius*, a.k.a. the Eastern coral snake, does not swim in the ocean among the sea coral.
- *Phrynosoma solare*, a.k.a. horned toad, is not a toad. It is a lizard.

Besides those names, it is certainly true that little alligator lizards are not alligators. Also, people from different places often use different common names for the same reptile. For example, some people in Africa call the Nile crocodile "mamba," but that is also a name for some African tree snakes!

So to very clearly name and group every known reptile species, herpetologists use an order for the groups to which each belongs. They classify reptiles first in very large groups and then smaller and smaller groups. From very general to specific, this is biology's order of living things: *kingdom, phylum, class, order, family, genus,* and *species.*

Read below and see how a garter snake is classified.

Classification of the Common Garter Snake

1. It is in the kingdom of the animals (*Animalia*), because it is not a plant or a fungus.
2. It is in the phylum *Chordata* because it has vertebrae.
3. It is in the class of the reptiles (*Reptilia*) because it is in this book!
4. It is in the order *Squamata* because it is grouped with the snakes and lizards.
5. It is in the family *Colubridae* because it is among a big group of common snakes that does not include rattlers or pythons.
6. It is in the genus *Thamnophis* because it is a garter snake.
7. It gets the species name *sirtalis* because it is the common garter, not the giant garter snake or the plains garter snake.

When you call a snake *Thamnophis sirtalis*, the name *sirtalis* tells you which *Thamnophis* snake you are talking about. You might say that scientific names for reptiles put the last name first like "Washington, George."

Since you know the prehistoric past of modern scaly creatures and how they fit into the animal kingdom, read on and go "back to class" with all the reptiles to learn more.

TryThis

A Memory Trick

You can memorize biology's group order for classifying living things: kingdom, phylum, class, order, family, genus, and species. The seven beginning letters to remember are K, P, C, O, F, G, and S. To remember them you can make up a silly sentence, like "Kind Phantoms Carry Old Fuzzy Gym Shoes."

FUN FACT

Tough Reptiles to Group

Amphisbaenians (not amphibians) are legless reptiles in the *Squamata* order but they are not snakes nor are they legless lizards.

The Four Orders in the Class of Reptilia

1. *Squamata* are the snakes and lizards
2. *Testudines* are the turtles and tortoises
3. *Crocodilia* are the crocodiles, alligators, caimans, and gharials
4. *Rhynchocephalia* is the lonely order just for the little tuataras!

Sensing in the Reptile World

When reptiles hunt or search for a mate, they sense the whole world differently than you do with the same five senses: sight, hearing, taste, touch, and smell. Many reptiles have a greater sense of smell and some have better eyesight than humans. Reptiles also use senses that human do not have.

Some Use the Five Senses Differently

Not all reptiles see the same. For example: Alligators have great vision for night hunting. Many lizards see very well, but most snakes do not see things far away very well and some are blind. Many snakes rely on other senses when they hunt.

Not all reptiles hear the same. Lizards and crocodilians hear the sounds that travel through the air. Snakes and turtles have no outside ears; they feel vibrations in their bodies that travel through the ground or water.

Snakes and many lizards like Gila monsters and monitors use their forked tongue to lick the air and deliver chemicals from the air to an organ in the roof of their mouth. They sense their surroundings in a way that is like both tasting and smelling. In some ways your senses of smell and taste are related too.

Other Reptile Senses

Reptiles have senses that herpetologists are still trying to understand. Adult tuataras and a few iguanas have a hidden light sensor beneath the scales on top of their head.

SUPER SENSES

Wouldn't it be cool to have another sense besides sight, smell, hearing, and touch? If you were a snake, you just might. Some snakes have a special organ that we don't have. See if you can figure out what it is by using this special decoder.

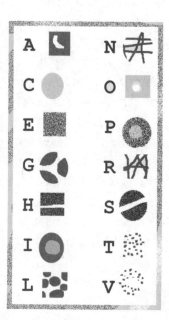

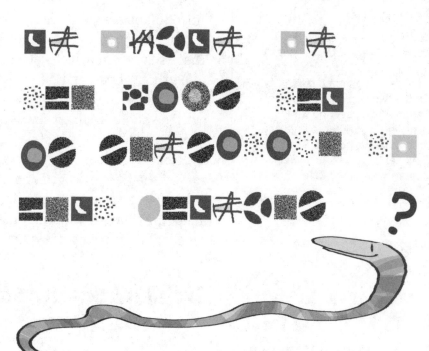

SEEING WITH YOUR NOSE

Some snakes have poor eyesight and rely on their sense of smell. Can you imagine getting around with your eyes half closed? Try it and see—you'll be bumping into all kinds of things. Which sense do you think you use the most?

This "third eye" is more noticeable when those reptiles are young, before scales cover it. Herpetologists guess it may sense the amount of ultraviolet light that those reptiles have absorbed. Could it be part of a sunbathing timer in their brains?

Crocodilians have mysterious sensors of their own that look like goose bumps on their scales. Gators and caimans have them only on their faces, and crocs have them on their entire bodies. Herpetologists think these bumps give crocodilians a way to sense where nearby prey is moving in muddy murky water where sight and smell do not help. These sensors may feel water movement made by fish.

Pythons, boas, and pit vipers use special heat sensor pits to locate their prey. You can find those sensor pits on pythons and boas lined across the top of their mouths. Every pit viper has just a pair of heat pits on its face. They appear to be extra nostrils but they are not. Pit vipers sense heat so well that herpetologists figure they have heat vision. The heat they sense from things around them may give them a moving thermal picture of their surroundings that is excellent for hunting down little warm-blooded creatures.

Excellent Energy Savers

Reptiles live in ways that save energy. Many prefer to wait for food to come to them. Many store up fat in their tails to survive long times without food. They can burst into action with great speed but only when necessary. Instead of calling them cold-blooded, you could call reptiles solar-powered. The sun gives their bodies the heat they need to stay active and digest food. They do not need to burn energy from the food they eat in order to keep their bodies warm. Being solar-powered is part of the reptile lifestyle.

Staying Warm and Coping with the Cold

Reptiles have ways to stay warm and the most basic way is *basking*. For example, a turtle will sit on a log to soak up the sun. A desert lizard will warm up on a rock to get ready to hunt. Some herpetologists think that the ridges on a croc's back help it soak up more heat when it basks in the sun.

When marine iguanas finish feeding in the ocean, they are very cold. They are black when they come out of the water to bask. That color change helps warm them. On a warm day try changing into a black shirt and then a white shirt and feel the difference. Black warms you up! Some snakes and lizards will seek the heat from black pavement on a road.

When the air turns cool in the evening, turtles and crocs take a nighttime swim to places where the waters are still warm. Water holds heat longer than the air.

When the seasons turn to fall and winter, many reptiles hibernate. The most amazing places to see reptiles rising from hibernation are the Narcisse Snake Pits of Manitoba, Canada. There you can witness red-sided garter snakes by thousands crawling over each other to exit their winter home and return to their warm season habitats. If you dislike snakes, it is not the place for you!

Handling the Heat

Sometimes the heat from the sun can be too much even for a reptile. That's why they have different ways to beat the heat. Many times they do what you do. They find shade or swim in cool waters. Some reptiles avoid going out in the daytime heat and hunt at night instead. Alligators seem to pant like puppies during the dog days of summer. They cannot let their tongues hang out but they do sit still with their mouths open wide to cool themselves. Gila monsters dig holes or borrow

TURTLE TRICK

It's a warm sunny day and these turtles are enjoying the warmth. But one of them doesn't belong. Can you see which one?

another animal's burrow for the hottest and driest times in the Mohave Desert. In a safe, cool place Gila monsters wait and become inactive without food until the desert heat is more bearable.

How Do Reptiles Behave?

The energy-saving reptiles do spend a lot of time just sitting, basking, and doing nothing. So how do herpetologists study reptile behavior if reptiles don't do anything? The truth is, reptiles do behave; they just don't frolic and play like mammals. Some reptile behavior to study involves active defense, reproduction, and communication.

Active Defense

A reptile's active defense is anything it does to stop a predator or make a predator go away. Biting is the first active defense for aggressive reptiles and the last active defense for shy reptiles like small lizards. For example, Eastern long-necked turtles can defend themselves quite well if picked up by the sides of their shells. They can turn around and bite the person who tries to pick them up that way.

Although a snake's main purpose for venom is hunting, cobras have developed fangs that allow them to defend themselves with venom in a special way. Cobra venom comes out of a hole on the lower front side of each fang instead of the bottom. Cobras can squirt venom out of those fangs, shake their heads, and spray it right at a predator's face.

Reptiles have some interesting ways to defend themselves. Hognose snakes will play dead. Musk turtles have glands that give off smelly liquid to make predators go away. Many lizards will drop their wiggling tails to escape predators and grow new tails. Many reptiles use speed as a defense. Many lizards prefer to run away from a fight. Small caimans have a special galloping run they use not for chasing prey but for escaping predators.

Reproduction

Scaly creatures have babies, and reptile reproduction gives herpetologists many behaviors to study. Males compete for the attention of females. Reptile parents mate. Some reptile mothers make nests. Then eggs hatch or babies are born.

Male reptiles duel in strange ways. Monitor lizards wrestle while standing on two feet. Competing black mamba snakes raise their heads several feet off the ground and seem to arm wrestle without arms. The winner presses the loser's head to the ground. Competing desert tortoises fight like cars in a very slow demolition derby contest. The winner flips the loser on his back. Male painted turtles try to swim face-to-face with a female, wave their front legs in front of her, and gently stroke her face with their claws.

After a male and female reptile mate, the female's eggs are fertilized. Females usually lay fertilized eggs with soft leathery shells, but not all reptile mothers lay their eggs. Some reptile mothers never lay their eggs in a nest. Instead they keep their eggs safe and warm inside their bodies until they are born. Common garter snakes do this. Whether a reptile egg is inside a nest or inside its mother, the egg carries all the food a baby reptile needs. Most mammals do not grow in eggs as reptiles do.

Reptile reproduction can be very surprising. For example, the temperature decides whether crocodilian and tuatara babies are male or female. While those reptile babies grow inside their eggs, the temperature of the nest near the top and bottom affects which ones become tiny males or tiny females. Eggs of many turtle species and a few lizard species are affected in much the same way. Imagine if the temperature of your house decided whether you would be a baby girl or a baby boy!

Among some rare reptiles there are no boys. Brahminy blind snakes are all females and their babies are identical female clones. Some herpetologists are studying lizards that will sometimes reproduce without males.

WORDS to KNOW

OVIPAROUS: Most reptiles, like pythons, are *oviparous* because they lay eggs that grow outside the mother. Some reptiles, like boas, are *ovoviviparous* because they grow in eggs inside their mothers' bodies. Mammals are viviparous because they are fed by their mothers' bodies as they grow inside them.

Those lizards include some whiptails, basilisks, and even Komodo dragons.

Reptile Babies Grow Up Quickly

Reptile babies have no time to just be a kid. Soon after hatching or birth, reptiles will walk, crawl, climb, swim, and hunt on their own. Most reptiles follow a different parenting plan than most mammals. Mammals give birth to smaller numbers of babies, nurture them with mother's milk, and protect them. Parent protection is important for mammal survival. Many reptiles hatch or give birth to larger broods of offspring and leave them to survive on their own instincts. Great numbers of offspring are needed for reptiles to survive the many predators that eat baby snakes, lizards, turtles, and crocodilians.

Baby sea turtles that hatch and survive to become adults and lay their own eggs are little heroes. A mother sea turtle buries her clutch of eggs on a sandy seashore. Under the dark of night when their mother is long gone, the babies hatch and work together to dig their way out of the sand. Once above ground they must flap their way across the beach to reach the ocean waves before birds and crabs easily make a meal out of them. The survivors of that race then must hide from fish that feed on them. Finally the strong and lucky turtles that live to about six years old will migrate back thousands of miles to where the females will bury their eggs on the same shores where they themselves had hatched. They do all that work because long ago reptiles developed eggs for dry land instead of water.

Some Reptile Talk

Communication is another scaly creature behavior. Most reptiles communicate without voices. Snakes and turtles have no vocal cords in their throats to make sound vibrations. The hissing they make is the sound of air they force through their breathing tubes. Geckos use vocal cords to make special calls to claim their small territories. Crocodilians also have vocal cords. Gator habitats become

noisy when male gators look for a mate. Their loud low bellowing makes ripples and splashes in the water. Baby gators start chirping inside the egg to tell each other "Let's bust outta these stuffy shells" and to tell mother "Dig us out of here!" Gator mothers hear these calls and dig out their babies.

Reptiles communicate in many ways without voices. For example, in addition to bellowing, male gators sound off with a hard slap of their jaws against the water. This sound is a very loud POW! Besides the many displays that male lizards make for females saying "Look at me," reptiles also use their bodies to say, "Go away!" Lizards have ways of making themselves look bigger. A threatened cobra can spread open the ribs on its neck to make a large hood that is also meant to say, "I am big. Go away!"

The rattlesnakes say "Go away" with their rattles, and other snakes without rattles make similar sounds with their bodies to say the same thing. Some copperheads just rustle dry leaves with their tails. Some snakes with rough scales make a rasp sound by rubbing their coils together.

Super Camo!

Camouflage is an adaptation of passive defense that reptiles use. Passive defense means defending yourself without doing something. That is how camouflage works. Reptiles sit still and their scaly skin blends in with their surroundings. Because so many reptiles are colored in the greens, grays, browns, and tans of their habitats, they are very good at hiding from both their predators and their prey.

Reptiles Wear Disguises

Color is not the only thing that gives a reptile good camouflage. The shape of a reptile can help hide it as well. Here is how. When you were little you learned to quickly recognize your basic geometric shapes. Predators learn to quickly recognize the basic shapes that are their food. If a little reptile has a shape without clear edges, it is harder for

WORDS to KNOW

EGG TOOTH: A reptile has a special baby tooth for cutting its way out of its eggshell, but the "egg tooth" is on the baby reptile's nose and it is not a real tooth. It is a sharp hornlike scale that falls off not long after the reptile hatches.

FUN FACT

Gators and Crocs Are Good Moms

Crocodilians do some caring for their young in ways that no other reptiles do. They protect their nests, carry their babies in their mouths, and guard their babies for as long as a year.

CLEVER CAMO

This little mouse doesn't know it but he's in big trouble. It looks like somebody's camouflage is working very well. Connect the dots and see who is hiding here in plain sight.

What do you get if you cross a newborn snake with a basketball?

BABY BASKETBALL

a predator to spot. That is why some herpetologists think the thorns on an Australian thorny devil are great camo. The thorny devil is just as jagged as the desert ground. The matamata turtle of the South America's Amazon River has jagged edges all over its shell and body. Its wide head and long neck are disguised like a ragged leaf. A muddy matamata is hard to recognize as a turtle.

Color Can Also Say "Go Away"

Some reptiles have bright colors that give them no camouflage at all. Often the colors of these reptiles deliver a familiar reptile message: "Go away!" The bright contrast between the pink and black scales of the Gila monster may warn animals to go away because it is poisonous. A painted turtle is not poisonous, but some herpetologists guess that the bright pattern on its plastron may scare away some fish because it could be dangerous to them. A painted turtle swallowed alive by a large fish can thrash its claws and seriously hurt the insides of the fish. Poisonous coral snakes have a recognizable pattern of stripes that goes red, yellow, black, red, yellow, black . . . This should warn all who find them to go away.

Some harmless snakes and even legless lizards mimic the colors of venomous snakes. King snakes and milk snakes mimic the three colors of coral snakes. An old rhyme describes coral snakes—"red and yellow kills a fellow" and its mimickers—"red and black venom lack." But that rhyme will not help you in South America where a species of coral snake does not have its red stripes next to its yellow stripes.

Confusing Anatomy

A few species of reptiles have one more passive defense. They have built-in decoys that confuse their predators. For example, the thorny devil's main predators are birds, and the last thing a thorny devil wants is a bird pecking its head. Fortunately, the knob behind its head may help protect it. When threatened, a thorny devil tucks its head down to the ground and attacking birds sometimes mistake that big knob for its head.

TryThis

The Effect of a Gator's Bellow

Fill the sink with water. Strike a tuning fork against a block of wood and put the fork into the water while it is still vibrating and making its tone. Sound will move the water just like a gator's bellowing in a swamp or a lake.

FuN FACT

White Tummies in the Water

When underwater creatures look up at the surface of the water they see the light of the sun. The white scales on an alligator's belly make its form less dark against that light and improve the alligator's chances of diving down unnoticed upon a turtle or fish.

An Australian skink called the shingleback has a tail that looks like its head. When you look at it you may not know if it is going forward or backward. If a predator attacks the tail, the shingleback will have a better chance at running away and hiding.

Stay Curious

The more you learn about all the reptiles, the more questions you will have, like "How do chameleons change colors?" That means you are becoming a scientist. Biologists like herpetologists and paleontologists always have new questions: Were the dinosaurs warm- or cold-blooded? Why are the Galapagos tortoises so big when they live on islands where food is hard to find? How do migrating sea turtles find their way across the ocean without getting lost?

Chapter 7
Reptiles and People

While flipping channels on the television you are bound to see reptiles. You may hear a scary nature show call them "cold-blooded killers." You may catch a news report about a lost pet python on the loose. Or you may see a giant lizard named Godzilla destroy a city. Reptiles certainly inspire people to tell stories. Some are part true, some are true, and some are just fiction. For thousands of years people have repeated stories about scaly creatures. People today still tell modern myths about reptiles. Some of those stories are mistaken as true. Fortunately, some scientists are so inspired by the amazing reptiles you have met in this book that they make it their jobs to learn more about them. Some people are inspired by reptiles to make inventions and designs that imitate them. Both stories and studies of reptiles say a lot about human fear and fascination with scaly creatures.

Ancient Stories

You probably know a lot of the facts about real scaly creatures. You might now enjoy comparing real reptiles to those in a few old tales that involve snakes, lizards, turtles, and crocodiles.

Snake Tales

In stories, snakes are often the opposite of famous; they are infamous for doing bad things. The ancient Hebrew book of Genesis holds a great example. It is the Hebrew story of how God made the earth and how Adam and Eve lived in a perfect place called Eden. The trouble in that story all started when a snake spoke. The snake tricked Eve into eating fruit that she and Adam were told not to touch. Because Adam and Eve broke God's rule they had to leave the Garden of Eden. They should not have listened to the snake.

One snake did help a Hebrew hero scare an evil Egyptian king (the Pharaoh) in the Hebrew book of Exodus. Aaron came with Moses to tell the Pharaoh to let their people go from slavery. Aaron threw his staff on the ground and it turned into a snake. The Pharaoh's magicians also turned their staffs into snakes, but Aaron's snake ate them. Aaron's snake must have been an elapid!

J.K. Rowling, an author of modern magical stories, uses people's ancient fear of snake talk to begin the adventure in her Harry Potter books. The trouble for her hero starts in her first book when Harry Potter realizes that he can talk with snakes.

The ancient Greeks had a story of a horrible monster named Medusa with a hairstyle made of hissing snakes. One look at her ugliness could turn a person into stone. She was killed by Perseus, who spied her reflection in his shiny shield. Not long ago a cuter version of Medusa named Celia Mae appeared in the animated movie *Monsters, Inc.* She still had snake hair but she did get a date with a monster named Mike.

SNAKE STORIES

When people are afraid of something, they often invent stories that make the scary thing seem even scarier. Can you tell which of these myths is true or false?

A HOOP SNAKE SWALLOWS ITS TAIL AND ROLLS AFTER PEOPLE.

SOME SNAKES HAVE VERY LONG FANGS THAT FOLD BACK IN THEIR MOUTH WHEN NOT IN USE.

SNAKES CAN HYPNOTIZE THEIR PREY WITH THEIR EYES OR BODY MOVEMENTS.

RATTLESNAKES CAN'T HEAR ANYTHING; THEY RELY ON MOVEMENT AND SMELL.

what?

A MILK SNAKE IS ABLE TO MILK A COW.

SNAKE JAWS ARE NOT FUSED TOGETHER AT THE BASE, ALLOWING THEM TO OPEN TO A SIZE MUCH BIGGER THAN THEIR HEADS.

HIGH ESTEEM

In ancient Central America Quetzalcoatl, the mythical "plumed serpent," was worshipped as the "Master of Life."

Lizard Tales

Centuries before a little talking gecko began doing commercials for a company called GEICO, people had already invented imaginary lizards. Dragons are the world's favorite imaginary lizards. People in Europe and Asia both have ancient stories of dragons. In England they still tell the legend of Saint George, who rescued a village from a dragon that was eating all the young maidens. When the king's daughter was next in line for the dragon's lunch, Saint George killed the beast and saved the princess. In Asia, Chinese dragons are magical creatures said to bring good fortune instead of destruction. Chinese New Year parades still often include bright red dragons that dance and twist as watchers hope for good luck in the new year.

America has a not-so-old dragon story. The song "Puff the Magic Dragon" was sung by the group Peter, Paul, and Mary. The sad song tells of a boy who outgrows his imaginary dragon friend. Real lizards do not live forever, but they can live longer than your childhood.

Turtle Tales

After the story of the Garden of Eden, the Hebrew book of Genesis has another story about a great flood that destroyed the earth and a man named Noah who saved the earth's animals in his boat. The native Ojibwa people of America's Midwest have their own story of how the Creator made the world and later flooded it. But the hero of that story is a great turtle. The turtle let the people and animals who survived the flood grow a new world on his back.

The slow turtles of storybooks do seem much like real turtles. You must have heard the story of the Tortoise and the Hare. Hopefully you learned the story's wise advice: "Slow and steady wins the race." Storybook turtles are often wise.

HIDING IN PLAIN SIGHT

Scientists believe there are 2,700 species of snakes in the world. Most of them are very skilled at staying hidden when they want to. Just like the snakes here. Can you find the following names in this puzzle?*

BLACK
BOA
BULL
COBRA
CORAL
FOX
GARTER
RACER
RATTLE
TIGER
TREE
WATER

P	L	A	R	O	C	R
E	B	N	R	V	O	K
X	O	F	A	L	B	C
G	A	R	T	E	R	A
W	H	M	T	R	A	L
A	P	B	L	L	U	B
T	I	G	E	R	F	O
E	E	R	T	S	S	Q
R	A	C	E	R	P	V

What subject are snakes good at in school?

HISSSTORY!

Careful, some names might be upside down or backward.

REPTILE *REPTILIS*

Even the word *reptile* is interesting. It comes from the Latin word *reptilis*, which means "creeping." Can you figure out what other words start with REP?

REP _ _ _ _
TO DO AGAIN

REP _ _ _ _
TO EXCHANGE WITH A NEW ONE

REP _ _ _
TO TELL A STORY ON THE NEWS

REP _ _ _
TO LISTEN TO AGAIN

REP _ _ _
TO FIX

Maybe people think of turtles as wise because some real turtles live to be quite old. A great example of a wise old turtle is in Jon J. Muth's book called *The Three Questions*. It is really an old tale by Leo Tolstoy, but Muth's story has a curious boy meet a wise old turtle named Leo. Leo the turtle helps the boy discover what is most important in life.

An Egyptian Croc God

Another sort of flood in Egypt led to an ancient Egyptian belief in a crocodile god named Sobek. Every year the flooding waters of Egypt's Nile river nourished farm land but the great river's waters also carried the feared Nile crocodiles. So Sobek, the crocodile, became Egypt's water god responsible for the green plants that grew along the Nile. Egyptians had two temples where live crocodiles were kept to honor and represent Sobek. When these holy crocs died they were mummified. Wow, that sounds like an idea for a scary movie, *Night of the Living Crocodile Mummies*!

Real People-Eaters

Stories of huge snakes eating humans are hard to prove true. However, in some countries, washing clothes or watering livestock takes people into crocodile habitats. Muggers and Nile crocs are not picky eaters, and people do become their prey.

Modern Myths

Some people today still tell, and some still believe, strange stories about reptiles. Take the Loch Ness Monster, for instance. Some people still wonder if that reptile or dinosaur-type monster lurks in a deep loch, or lake, in Scotland. In America, where people cannot resist stories like Bigfoot, some people in Wisconsin and South Carolina instead claim their Lizard Man stories are real. If those stories of a half-man, half-lizard creature are true, then which state is really Lizard Man's home? Years ago in the southwest of the United States people thought horned lizards could spit blood right into your eyes and make you blind like a cobra can with its venom. In New York City, some people have said baby alligators flushed down into the sewer have grown large down there below the streets. The truth is that alligators could never survive in sewer water.

A fantastic reptile story in the United States comes from Florida, but this story is real. The reports and photographs of giant pythons living in the Everglades and giant pythons challenging alligators are true. These pythons once were pets and later were abandoned in the wild, and now are reproducing in their new home. Pythons are alien species in the United States, and Florida wildlife workers are dealing with a serious alien invasion!

Reptile Science

Thank goodness some bright and curious people make it part of their jobs to know the facts about reptiles. People get involved in herpetology in many ways. Some people work with reptiles in zoos. Some are biologists doing genetic research. Some are professors in universities. Some are managers of wildlife outdoors. For example, in her job, Professor Colleen Farmer of the University of Utah has learned new things about how crocodiles and alligators can digest large prey, breathe while they run, and control their swimming with the air in their lungs.

FUN FACT

Rattlers Don't Tell Their Age

Since a rattlesnake adds a knob to its rattle each time it sheds, you may have heard you can tell its age by counting knobs on its rattle. However, not all rattlers shed their skin the same number of times each year, and those knobs often do break off.

WORDS to KNOW

IRONIC: Something opposite of what you would expect is ironic. Teenage Mutant Ninja Turtles are ironic, because real turtles are slow but these are fast superheroes. And, ironically, they need a wise teacher while storybook turtles are often wise themselves.

Making Reptile Design Inventions

Some adaptations that reptiles have are so useful that scientists study them to learn how to copy them and use them for inventions to serve people. For example, if scientists can learn how the skin on the Australian thorny devil can send water to the thorny devil's mouth, then they may be able to invent new materials that can easily collect water.

At the University of Maryland, Professor Satyandra Gupta and his students have worked to design robots that move like snakes. Such robots could be very good at going places where other robots cannot go, like tunnels and narrow spaces. Very small snake robots could be used to help doctors do surgery.

Even artists are inspired to make reptile art. Michael Sweere is an artist in Minnesota who makes art using recycled materials like cereal boxes, broken dishes, and old tin. Colorful snakes are something he enjoys making with bottle caps or baby food jar lids. With some help from an adult, some tools, and some wire from the hardware store, you too might enjoy making a metal rattlesnake like Michael's.

TWO HEADS ARE BETTER THAN ONE

Another myth is that snakes don't have bones. Of course this is untrue, as we can see from snake skeletons. But looking at these mythical two-headed snakes you can see why people might think they have no bones. How many two-headed snakes can you find here?

TryThis

Share Reptile Info with Friends

You can make reptile trading cards. Cut cereal boxes into rectangles. A good size is 4" × 3". Roughen the cards' shiny sides with sandpaper before gluing on pictures of favorite reptiles you draw or find. Before you wrap each durable card with clear packing tape, record fun facts about each reptile on the back.

More Reptile Discoveries to Make

Fact is often more amazing than fiction. Herpetology can be just as fascinating as legends, because in herpetology there is always something more to learn. Some scientists are looking for cures for human illnesses in snake venom. Others are examining crocodile blood to capture and imitate the crocodile's strong ability to fight germs. Since seeing is believing, learn about real reptiles by seeing them in the wild, in zoos, or with some select reptiles as pets.

Chapter 8

Owning Your Own Reptile

With all that you know now about reptiles, you may be very curious about them. Maybe you have visited reptiles at the zoo. Maybe you have spied on reptiles in the wild. And now you may want a reptile as a pet in your own home. Imagine how much you could learn if you closely cared for a snake, a lizard, or a turtle!

A Lasting Relationship

Becoming a pet owner is a commitment. Owning a scaly ectothermic pet is a special commitment. If you bring a reptile home and properly care for it, you will have a happy healthy reptile. You will learn about a reptile up close and personally! You may proudly say that you have a pet different than most in your neighborhood. However, if you are not prepared or not committed to caring for your pet, it may get sick or live a short life.

Many reptiles live long lives. Consider these examples.

LIFE EXPECTANCIES FOR SOME REPTILES YOU KNOW

SPECIES	YEARS
COMMON GARTER SNAKE	ABOUT 10
GREEN IGUANA	ABOUT 15
COMMON BOA	ABOUT 30
COMMON SNAPPING TURTLE	ABOUT 50
AMERICAN ALLIGATOR	ABOUT 50

Do not let the small size of some pet reptiles fool you; they too can live a long time. A pet hamster may live two

WORDS to KNOW

LIFE EXPECTANCY: An animal's life expectancy is the number of years you can expect it to live. The life expectancy for a wild reptile often differs from a captive one, because life as a pet or in a zoo is not the same as life in a natural habitat.

or three years, but owning a pet reptile could be your job for a much longer time. Even though pet stores display snakes, lizards, and turtles in glass tanks much like hamsters and gerbils, most reptile pets should outlive such small fuzzy pets. For that reason, before you buy a reptile you should make plans for a long and lasting relationship with your scaly critter.

Some people may think that a reptile is an unusual pet, but a young person like you can successfully care for one. Of course, many reptiles do not make good pets; if you dream of owning a sea turtle, alligator, Gila monster, or rattlesnake, please just get a toy one. Fortunately, some reptiles really do make excellent pets.

Do Your Homework First

If you want a mellow pet that won't chew your slippers, a reptile may be for you. Living with a reptile is different than living with a cat or dog. A reptile is a very quiet pet. It does not leave fur on your furniture. You will not need to take it for early morning walks. A pet reptile will not demand your attention the way cats or dogs do.

Your pet reptile will have its own special needs. Tuning in to and caring for those needs will be new for you. Prepare yourself with as much information as you can collect.

Do your homework before buying your reptile. Read books about keeping reptiles—good news, you are doing that already! Seek out people for firsthand advice. Most people love to talk about their pets. If you are lucky enough to know a reptile owner, quiz her as much as you can or ask him about success and failure he has had while caring for his pet. Ask, "How much time do you give to your reptile?" You can learn from other people's mistakes and repeat their successes.

Next, before you buy make sure you have "backup." Speak with friends, neighbors, cousins, aunts, uncles, or other relatives who also think reptiles are cool. Tell them you are getting one soon. Tell them you are going to get

FUN FACT

Time Is Money

You'll need to save some time and money to care for a reptile. Spending time every day, even a little, caring for your herp will make it happy and make you a very responsible person!

HAPPY HABITAT

Paul has made a maze in case his pet snake Sammy gets bored. Can you see how Sammy can get from the hanging branch to his water dish?

HISS KISS   What does a snake sign at the bottom of his letters?

a really cute one! Then ask these people if they would be willing to care for your little reptile while you are gone, because a day will come when you and your family go on a vacation or a visit where your reptile may not follow. Also, find a veterinarian near you who is experienced with treating reptiles. Not all vets know reptiles as well as other pets. The time to look for a good vet for your reptile is before your reptile gets sick. Sooner or later all pet owners have questions for the vet.

Finally, find a good place to buy your new pet. Two choices are best: either a pet store with people who understand reptiles and take time to talk with young customers, or a herpetological society that places rescued reptiles in adoptive homes. Maybe your local herp society does this. Going out into the hills, ponds, or desert near your home to find a wild reptile is not the proper way to get a pet.

Again, whether at the pet store or at a herpetological society meeting, ask more questions. Ask pet store workers when their young reptiles were born or hatched. That way you can learn how they get their reptiles. A captive-bred reptile with a known history is a good choice. Also, at a herpetological society, ask and be sure that a rescued reptile is healthy, not injured or in need of special care. You want to find the healthiest reptile for your pet.

Making a Habitat for Your Pet

Before you bring your reptile home, make sure you have a container ready. Since you are just getting started, you want to keep it simple. Since you want to give your reptile room to grow, you will need a container that is large enough. A common container for a reptile is a twenty-gallon glass tank, much like a big fish tank. What you will like about that tank is how simple it is to clean. You will also enjoy clearly seeing your pet inside it. Make sure the tank has a screened lid that closes tightly and securely. You do not want your reptile to escape!

WORDS to KNOW

CAPTIVE-BRED: Chickens are hatched from mothers that were raised by humans. So too are captive-bred reptiles.

WORDS to KNOW

ALIEN REPTILES: Alien reptiles are not from another planet! Alien species are wild animals living in new places because people moved them there on purpose or accidentally. For example, Africa's Jackson's chameleon now also lives quite well in Hawaii. That species is an alien to Hawaii. It arrived there in the 1970s when some of them escaped from pet owners.

Where Do You Put This Glass Tank?

Like Goldilocks said, "Not too hot and not too cold." Follow her advice for your sensitive ectothermic pet. Right in front of a window may not be the place for your reptile. Too much direct sunlight can easily heat up a glass reptile tank like a parked car on a hot day. However, being in a room that does get some sunlight is good for your reptile. Also, stay clear of drafty windows, doors, or other places that will expose your reptile to cold air.

After temperature, think of vibrations too. Tortoises and snakes in particular feel sound with their bodies. Remember that and place your reptile away from the television, stereo, or washing machine. Close and constant rumbling or blaring from a nearby appliance could disturb your reptile.

Finally, if you already live with a cat, a dog, or a curious little brother or sister, place your reptile's tank somewhere safe from their reach. In fact, before you buy a reptile or anything for it, talk with a vet or someone at a herpetological society meeting and describe for them the persons and creatures who already live in your home. Some animals carry germs that are harmful to certain reptiles. More importantly, reptile pets should be not live with pregnant mothers and very young children who have not grown strong defenses against germs.

Plan for Your Reptile's Basic Needs

Many keepers of reptiles carefully prepare containers for their reptiles with plants, rocks, and wet or dry spaces that look and feel much like the natural habitats of the species they own. Some folks enjoy making a mini-jungle or desert! Watching a reptile in such a container gives you the feeling of traveling into another world, much like a large aquarium of tropical fish can do. Actually, a natural-looking reptile tank like this has a name similar to the word aquarium. It is called a *vivarium*.

You will not start out with a fancy vivarium for your reptile. You will prepare a simple container that supplies the

ZOONOSES: Zoonoses are not the noses you see at the zoo. A zoonosis is a disease or sickness caused by germs passed between animals and people.

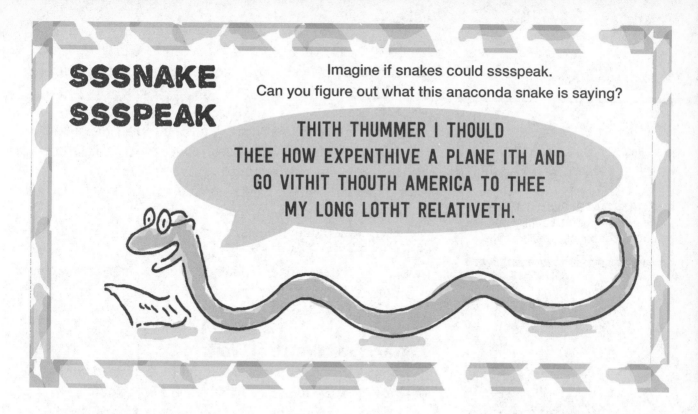

SSSNAKE SSSPEAK

Imagine if snakes could sssspeak.
Can you figure out what this anaconda snake is saying?

THITH THUMMER I THOULD
THEE HOW EXPENTHIVE A PLANE ITH AND
GO VITHIT THOUTH AMERICA TO THEE
MY LONG LOTHT RELATIVETH.

basic needs of your reptile and you will learn to maintain that before you add the extras. So what are the basics?

Your Reptile's Basic Needs
- clean bedding where it crawls and goes to the bathroom
- a place to drink
- a place to eat
- a place to hide
- controlled heat to maintain its body temperature
- ultraviolet light to stay healthy

Start with bedding on the bottom of your reptile's tank. A dog does not enjoy running on a smooth wood floor and your reptile does not want to crawl on the slippery bottom of its tank. Give your reptile bedding on which to move. The bedding can be as simple as paper towels or newspaper for a young lizard or small snake. The bedding can also be pine shavings, tree bark, alfalfa pellets, or sand. Your pet store can explain what bedding is best for your reptile.

WORDS to KNOW

ULTRAVIOLET LIGHT: You cannot see ultraviolet (UV) light, but your body feels it. To stay healthy your body and a reptile's body both need some, but not too much, of this light to make vitamin D.

Your reptile will need a shallow bowl of water. A snake can lift its head over and into a medium-sized bowl. A lizard or turtle will need a shallower bowl in order to lean in and take a drink. Choose a clay bowl that is too heavy for your pet to tip over.

If your reptile is a herbivore you will need a bowl or feed rack for the plants and vegetables you feed it. If your reptile is a carnivore, consider getting a separate container where you can put your reptile when it is time to feed it.

Next think of how secure you felt when you have found your own little hiding place to read a book. You will need to make a hiding place for your reptile. Your reptile may be small enough to go under a plastic food container, or you can buy many sorts of hiding places at the pet store. Be sure to use something washable.

You Have Electrical Work to Do

Your reptile needs lamps. Most pet reptiles need lamps for three reasons. Some need visible light in the daytime; some need more invisible ultraviolet light; and most need the steady warmth of an overhead lamp. You will not find one lamp that can do it all. For ultraviolet light get a fluorescent lamp made for reptiles, not for growing plants. That lamp will not warm your reptile, but it should be turned on during the daytime next to a hot incandescent bulb. When you go to bed is when your reptile needs a nighttime lamp on the other end of its tank. The nighttime lamp needs a special red, blue, or black bulb that makes heat but no noticeable light that would disturb your reptile.

You will learn a lot about light bulbs as you care for your reptile. Shop for them and examine them at the pet store. Work with an adult to use them safely. Be sure your lamps can handle the size (wattage) light bulbs you use. Your hot lamp's plug for the bulb should be ceramic. Plastic will melt. Don't leave your daytime light on twenty-four hours a day. You wouldn't like your bedroom light on all the time and neither would your reptile. Make sure that your hot lamp is always (day or night) on one end of your reptile's tank so your reptile can move from end to end to enter the heat or

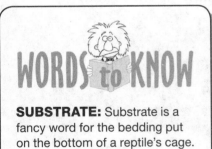

HOME SWEET CAVE

When you're making a home for your pet, make it as safe and comfortable as possible. This little snake escaped and is trying to find shelter from the big storm coming. But he has to be careful—only one of the caves is empty. Can you tell which one?

The empty cave is in a row with a teacup.
The empty cave is not below a boot.
The empty cave is not above a boot.

ARE YOU THERE?

Snakes are just one of many animals (including beetles, caterpillars, moths, lizards, and frogs) that use camouflage to hide.

leave the heat. If the hot lamp is above the middle of the tank, your reptile will not be able to escape the heat and it will overheat. Finally, a thermometer for checking the temperature in your tank is a must.

Feeding Your New Pet

When you were a baby your parents spent time feeding you and learning HOW to feed you. Think of your new reptile as your new baby. You will learn to feed your "baby" right. Feeding any reptile is not a quick rip-open-a-bag or a crack-open-a-can sort of job. If your reptile is a carnivore, it will eat frozen or fresh critters. If you get a herbivore, you will become very good at making salads! If your reptile is an omnivore you will be preparing a menu of both small critters and crunchy plants.

What's on the Menu?

Here are a few common foods for reptiles.

- **Rodents:** Your carnivore may eat tiny baby mice or someday may grow large enough to eat a rabbit. For a young keeper of reptiles, frozen rodents whether big or small are a better choice than live rodents.
- **Crickets:** These will be live bugs. If your carnivore eats crickets, you will learn how to care for live bugs as well as a live reptile!
- **Greens:** Your herbivore will eat lots of green leafy food like carrot tops and collard greens. The pale iceberg lettuce you find on fast food burgers and tacos is not a good green for your herbivore (or you) because it has very few nutrients.
- **Vegetables:** Besides lots of greens, your herbivore will need a few veggies. Good veggies for your herbivore may include squash, zucchini, and sweet potatoes.

When caring for a carnivore, remember that its food will need to grow as it grows. You may have a lizard that will first need crickets but later need mice. Or you may have a

WORDS to KNOW

INCANDESCENT BULB: Thomas Edison invented the incandescent bulb. Inside it, electricity flows through a tiny wire that glows and gets hot. A fluorescent bulb does not get hot. It sends electricity through a gas that emits ultraviolet (UV) rays. Those UV rays make chemicals on the glass of the bulb glow.

snake that first eats very small pink hairless mice called "pinkies," then slightly bigger ones called "fuzzies," later large adult mice, and finally small rabbits. So a reptile needs to graduate to bigger foods to grow a strong healthy jaw, much like when you gave up baby food long ago.

If your reptile is a cricket-eater, remember a couple of important things. First, feeding your pet starving crickets will starve your pet. Half-dead crickets do not have the nutrients your reptile needs. When you buy crickets, buy food for them too. Here is a second piece of cricket advice. Have you ever listened to their soothing song outside your bedroom window? That chirping may not help you sleep if it is coming from inside your bedroom. Store your crickets someplace where their noise will not disturb you or anyone else at night.

Before you take home a herbivore, do this special homework. Make three lists of foods related to the reptile you choose. Call the first list "Lots of These." Call the second list "Some or Just a Little." Call the third list "None of These Please." Get help from books, friends, pet stores, and the vet to learn what plants go on each of your three lists. You will learn a lot about plants as you feed a healthy herbivore. One thing you will learn is this: Some plants that are good for you are not good for your herbivore.

When the Dinner Bell Rings

Suppose you already have your pet reptile and its food. Maybe you have the vegetable drawer in the fridge stuffed with fresh greens. Maybe you have a container full of well-fed crickets. Maybe you have permission from your family to store a plastic bag of pinkies in a chosen spot in the freezer. What now?

At your herbivore's dinner time, rotating and chopping will be important. First, rotate the greens and veggies you give your reptile. That means serving a regular variety of plant food instead of always feeding the same things. With a variety of plants your herbivore gets more of the nutrients it needs and less of some that are not so good. Second, chop the greens and veggies to make them easier to eat. Your

Hickory Dickory
Deeezer . . .

. . . How long can mice stay in the freezer? Frozen mice, rats, or rabbits can be kept in the freezer for about four to five months before your carnivore eats them.

Two Things Your Reptile Does Not Want from You

If you have bug spray or hand lotion on your hands when you handle your reptile those chemicals can harm your pet. So always wash your hands before you handle your reptile.

parents did it for you when you were little; now do the same favor for your little reptile!

Dinnertime for your carnivore will be training time for you. You read earlier about putting a snake into a different container before feeding it. It is a good routine to follow. This helps communicate to a pet when feeding time is ON and when feeding time is OFF. If you give your reptile predictable signs that tell it when to expect food, you will have a reptile with predictable behavior. It will be less likely to bite you or others who handle it. This is the reason you will not feed your reptile outside its tank or its feeding container. Do not hold or handle your pet while it eats. Give your reptile some space to itself during dinner.

Good news! You do not need to be a chef to prepare frozen rodents for your carnivore. Cooked food is not good for a reptile. You will not use hot water or the microwave to thaw them out. You will thaw them out at room temperature. After the rodent is unfrozen your carnivore may also appreciate you wiping it dry before serving it.

Safe and Clean

You and your pet reptile are made of millions and millions of cells, the tiny building blocks for living creatures. The world is also full of tiny one-cell creatures called *bacteria*. They are everywhere: in the dirt, on your reptile, on your skin, and in your stomach. Some bacteria do good things like making rich soil for plants or tasty yogurt for you. However, some bacteria are germs that make us sick. Some germs in your reptile's tank can harm your pet, and some germs on your reptile are not good for you. The germs you need to fight are in reptiles' waste (pee and poop).

Germ Fighting

Think of your bathroom. Even though your family keeps it clean, you would never eat or sleep in there. Your reptile, however, will live in one room where it does everything including going to the bathroom. It cannot get away from its own waste, so you take it away. When you see a poop in the tank, you use a paper towel to remove it. Your reptile might use the water dish as a toilet, so at least once a day you empty the water dish, rinse it, scrub it with a paper towel, and refill it with fresh water. Change the bedding in the tank often. All these things will help fight germs in your pet's tank.

There are two more things you can do to fight germs. Remember WHB and WHA. Always "Wash Hands Before" and "Wash Hands After" you handle your reptile or anything in its tank. Wash your hands before you handle your reptile because you may carry germs that make your reptile sick. Wash your hands after handling your reptile and after cleaning its home to avoid getting sick yourself. Remember zoonoses make people or animals sick when germs are shared.

Salmonella is a zoonosis you should know. Reptiles and other animals often carry salmonella bacteria but do not get sick from it. Salmonella can make people sick. You need not worry about salmonella if you keep your reptile's tank clean and always WHA handling your pet. Do not kiss your reptile no matter how cute it is! Pet reptiles should stay out of the kitchen or any place where you eat or store people food. This is all about being safe and clean.

Shedding Skin Is Less Trouble Than Shedding Fur

Shedding causes hairy problems for dog and cat owners but much less worry for reptile owners. Shedding skin is a normal process that reptiles should do several times a year. A younger reptile that is growing more quickly will shed more than a slow growing adult. If your reptile is not shedding, take it to the vet to find out if it is sick. Your reptile will handle most of its shedding work on its own but you may need to help with troublesome old skin that hangs on. Old skin that refuses to let go of a snake's tail or a lizard's toes can cut off blood flow to those body parts. To rescue a tail and toes from old dry skin, give your reptile moisture. A spray of water, a wrap in a wet towel, or short dip in shallow

FUN FACT

Snakes Have Goggles When They Shed

The old scales, or eye caps, that protect a snake's eyes come off with the rest of a snake's shed skin. Often the shed eye caps come off looking like goggles.

water can moisten and loosen old skin. Having a hide box that holds some moisture helps during shedding time. If your reptile has trouble shedding skin on or around its eyes, see a vet for help.

Duties of a Young Herpetologist

Kindness, curiosity, and caution also play a part in the safety of your pet. First, for safety's sake and for goodness' sake, be kind to your reptile. It is living creature, not a toy. Treat it gently and learn the proper way to handle it.

Be curious. Herpetologists observe closely and often wonder. If you do the same, you will notice changes in your pet that others will overlook. You will notice that your pet is not just a living reptile but a unique one that will act in its own ways. Changes in its behavior or looks will be its signs of health or illness. You may have questions about whether or not your reptile will need to hibernate. You will have many "why" questions, much like when you did when you were little. Enjoy that curiosity.

Be cautious. Do not let your curiosity lead you to experiment on your pet. For example, putting another live animal into your pet's tank just to see what will happen is not a good idea. Do not feed wild mice or birds to a pet snake. Why? They may pass germs to your pet. Even live mice purchased from a store are risky for a reptile. Why? When reptiles hunt in the wild their prey tries to run away. When a reptile goes after live prey in a container the prey is more likely to fight back because it is trapped with your pet.

If keeping a reptile does not work out for you, please take time to find your pet a new owner. Talk to friends and family again, post an ad, and tell your teacher you are looking for a new home for a good pet. Do not leave your reptile outside somewhere to find a home in the wild. Either your reptile will die in a habitat where it cannot survive or it may survive and threaten other native species in your local habitats. If you simply cannot find a new home yourself please contact a herpetological society where some members may be able to take in your reptile.

Chapter 9

Six Super Reptiles for Beginners

If you are ready for a reptile, you will want one that is safe and simple to handle. You want a pet you can enjoy. However, caring for some reptiles is difficult. Some aggressive snakes do not want to be held in your hands. A tail-whipping lizard can give you a nasty cut. Some geckos with fragile skin cannot be handled much at all by their keepers. Keeping chameleons is complicated. Housing aquatic turtles is messy and stinky. Iguanas grow large enough to need a room of their own. So what can a beginner bring home? You could consider one of two good-looking snakes. You could get one great little gecko. You could tame a dragon! You might think of buying a skink. Or, you might meet the challenge of caring for a special tortoise . . . but not the Galapagos kind. Each of these reptiles can be handled by a young herpetologist like you who understands the basics of feeding, housing, and cleaning up after reptiles.

Corn Snakes and King Snakes

If you want a beautiful pet, consider the corn snakes and king snakes. Corn snakes are colored in a warm mosaic of gold, brown, and orange scales. They are one of the most popular pet snakes in the United States. King snakes may not be as popular in the homes and classrooms of children, but they are equally beautiful with their brilliant bands of color. Finding a captive-bred corn snake or king snake is no problem, since many are raised by breeders every year.

Many also are bred into different variations of their natural color patterns. People have even called some of these pets "designer snakes."

Corn snakes and king snakes are both diurnal. Both feed well in captivity compared to many other snakes. Even though adult corn snakes can grow to an adult length close to five feet, they respond very well to handling. King snakes do not grow as large, but they take longer to adjust to handling. Before a young king snake adjusts to being held in your hands you are bound to get peed and pooped on more than a few times.

When handling your snake, it will become used to you as you become confident holding it. Touching your snake first before removing it from its container for handling is a routine that tells your pet when it is not feeding time. Although you can pick up a baby corn or king snake with one hand, you should use two hands to pick up an adult. When your parent used to pick you up you were held and supported at your head and back. Do the same for your snake. Hold the adult snake firmly behind the head and under its middle.

Some things to add into your corn snake's tank are a large water dish and a secure climbing branch. Your snake may bathe itself in its dish. This can help moisten and loosen skin when shedding. Sometimes a snake will leave its waste in its water dish. Yes, yuck, but that makes your cleanup easier because then you do not have to empty the tank and replace the substrate. Just clean and refill the water dish often. You can give your corn snake a place to climb with a branch that goes diagonally across the tank. Make sure both ends are secured into corners of the tank so the branch stays put.

Corn snakes come from temperate climates in the United States. They do not live in hot deserts or extreme cold, but in the wild they do hibernate when the temperature drops. So if you do not want your corn snake to slip into hibernation, be sure to keep steady control of the temperature and light

AGGRESSIVE: Defensive species tend to hide or run when they feel threatened, while aggressive species tend to strike and fight. Over time and with proper handling your reptile will be calm when it sees you and relaxed when you hold it.

in its tank if winter begins to cool your house and shorten your daylight hours. Some keepers of corn snakes do let them hibernate, but as a beginner you may want to avoid working your snake through hibernation when you are still getting to know it.

With proper care your king snake could live ten to fifteen years and your corn snake could live up to twenty years.

Leopard Gecko

If you want a cute little lizard, you will like a leopard gecko. Leopard geckos grow to about seven inches long. They do not develop their bold leopard spots until they are adults. When they are young they have dark bands of color across their bodies.

You may be disappointed to learn that the leopard gecko does not have large toe pads and the ability to climb the glass of its tank, but it can climb and it is a tough gecko. For example, unlike some other geckos, it does not have fragile skin that can be easily damaged when touched by a handler. That means the leopard gecko is a little reptile that you can enjoy holding safely.

When handling your gecko, calmly scoop it up with two hands. Do not pick your gecko up by its tail, because your gecko will then drop its tail and the new tail will never look the same as the original. Be sure to hold your gecko low enough over its tank, a couch, or the floor so in case it falls from your hands it will not be hurt. If you have ever "walked" a hamster in your hands then you have practiced a good technique for holding your gecko. Let it crawl from your one hand to the other and continue putting your empty hand in front of your gecko to provide for its next step. After a while your gecko will relax in your hand.

Then you will notice how different this reptile feels. Like a normal reptile its skin is dry, but the leopard gecko's skin feels soft and loose like a leopard frog. Its skin in some places is almost see-through.

Another reason to not hold your leopard gecko too high above the floor is its natural habitat. Wild leopard geckos live mostly on the ground in the deserts of Pakistan, not high in the trees of the tropics. Pet geckos now are nearly all bred in captivity.

Despite being a desert reptile, your leopard gecko will need some humidity. The hide place you make for your gecko is where you give it moisture needed to properly shed old skin. Cut an entrance hole in the side of a plastic deli container. Put some moist sphagnum moss into the container and put back on the lid. Put this hiding container upside down on the floor of the gecko's tank. Be sure to moisten the moss again when it gets dry and replace it when it spoils.

Your gecko's large eyes tell you it is nocturnal. As a young hunter it will hunt about three to four dozen crickets a week. Remember to feed the crickets food too and find

FUN FACT

Watch for Your Snake's Cloudy Grumpy Eyes

When your snake's bright eyes get a cloudy blue glaze, this is a sign that your snake will soon shed. Many snakes don't want to be handled around that time. Don't worry. After shedding, your snake will look brand new and act like its old self again.

SELECTIVE SNAKE

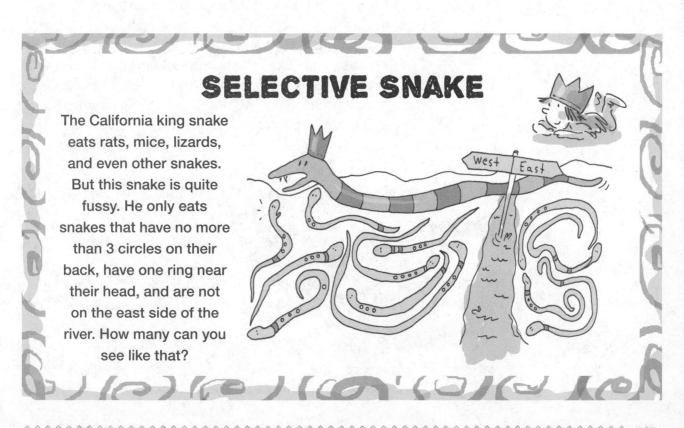

The California king snake eats rats, mice, lizards, and even other snakes. But this snake is quite fussy. He only eats snakes that have no more than 3 circles on their back, have one ring near their head, and are not on the east side of the river. How many can you see like that?

West   East

calcium supplement powder to sprinkle on the crickets for the health of your gecko. You will enjoy watching your gecko pounce on its tiny prey!

You may think that since leopard geckos are small, getting two would be not much more trouble. Instead, please stick with one gecko while learning the ins and outs of care. Two male geckos in the same tank lead to fights. A male and female in the same tank could lead to more geckos than you want.

With proper care your leopard gecko could live up to fifteen years.

Bearded Dragon

If you want a lizard that is a step up in size, then bring home a "beardie." The most common pet dragon is the inland bearded dragon. Captive-bred beardies are easy to find. An adult beardie may grow to twenty inches long.

Handling a young beardie is done much like walking a gecko in your hands. Also as is the rule with the gecko, so is the rule with the beardie: Do not pick up it up by the tail. However, your beardie has a feel all its own. Its scales are prickly. Its toes are like little hooks. Holding your beardie will not hurt, just feel strange at first. Later when your beardie gets to be a biggie, handling it will be exciting because it no longer fits inside your hand and it climbs onto your clothes.

WORDS to KNOW

HEATING PAD: An electrical-powered heating pad can be stuck on the glass beneath your tank on the same side as your night lamp. It supplies an extra heat source for your beardie or your blue-tongue but it cannot replace a heat bulb. Read ALL the pad's directions before you install it.

SCAREDY SKINK

Skinks have two different ways of defending themselves. One is to drop their tails (so they can escape with the predator holding their tail!) and the other is by using camouflage. How many times can you see the word SKINK hidden here?

W	I	S	S	I	K	W	I	N	J
K	W	I	Y	K	K	J	H	I	I
S	K	I	N	K	I	Z	I	K	I
S	K	I	N	S	S	K	O	K	K
S	I	N	S	K	I	S	S	I	S
K	K	I	N	I	N	W	I	S	
I	N	I	S	K	I	N	K	N	K
N	H	I	V	I	S	K	I	E	I
K	L	O	W	I	N	K	N	O	N
H	I	V	I	S	S	K	U	I	K
S	K	I	N	K	H	I	K	S	S

SKINK FANS

Blue-tongued skinks are a very popular pet. In fact, they even have their own website: www.bluetongueskinks.net.

Be careful to keep your beardie off the curtains. Getting it down will not be easy.

Choosing this larger reptile means some added cost and responsibility. First, you will need a bigger tank, usually a forty-gallon tank. Your big beardie will need more floor space for exercise. While your beardie is still small you can install a dividing wall in the middle of the tank to cut down your tank cleaning work. When your beardie is bigger, remove the divider and add a climbing branch.

Second, you may have to work more to keep the substrate and tank floor clean and dry, because beardies are diggers from the dry lands of Australia. If your substrate is flat newspaper, your beardie may wiggle beneath the paper and leave its mess right on the glass. Bad beardie! You can instead use fluffy newspaper mulch, but it will soak up moisture if your house is humid. Your beardie cannot have a soggy substrate. You may replace bedding often or haul a dehumidifier into the beardie's room.

Third, when your beardie blinks at you with its funny little eyes that say "Feed me," you need to be ready and know that beardies are omnivores! Do the food homework explained in Chapter 8. You will have menu planning to do. With proper care, your bearded dragon could live up to ten years.

Blue-Tongued Skink

If you want to freak out your friends, the appearance of a blue-tongued skink might do it. Many blue-tongues can grow up to two feet long. A blue-tongue's body is also wide. It has a large head and thick tail. Its smooth scales overlap like those of the corn snake. When its piercing eyes blink and follow you it is quite a sight, but nothing compared to its big blue tongue.

TORTOISE TRICKS

The Russian tortoise is known by lots of different names. Which ones do you think are real?

RUSSIAN BOX TURTLE

AFGHANISTAN TORTOISE

YELLOW-BELLIED TORTOISE

NINJA TORTOISE

FOUR-TOED TORTOISE

ONE-HUMP TORTOISE

STEPPE TORTOISE

COOL KAZAKHSTAN TORTOISE

THE LONG AND SHORT OF IT

The best way to tell a male tortoise from a female tortoise is by looking at the tail. The male has a longer tail that curves to the side.

270 AND COUNTING

It is estimated that there are 270 species of turtles in the world. Maybe you could find a new one and have it named after you!

INTRODUCING... ASHLEE!!

Like the beardie, the blue-tongue is an omnivore from Australia and will need a large tank, forty-gallon size or greater. It will enjoy a climbing branch. Like the leopard gecko, it will do well to have moist sphagnum moss in its hiding place.

With proper care your blue-tongued skink could live up to twenty years.

Russian Tortoise

If you and your family are ready to begin a big commitment, then you can consider a Russian tortoise. Finding a healthy captive-bred Russian tortoise will require some searching; try a trusted pet store, or a breeder with a good reputation.

This small tortoise grows only to about eight inches long, but it is a big responsibility. The Russian tortoise is another powerful digger. It needs deeper substrate in a cage or tank with plenty of roaming space on the floor. Tortoises benefit from time outside when the weather allows. The Russian tortoise needs to hibernate, so you will need to prepare a hibernation box for your tortoise. You will learn to judge your tortoise's health and readiness for hibernation. Sick tortoises do not hibernate well.

The Russian tortoise is a lively herbivore that can learn to eat out of your hands. With proper care, your Russian tortoise could live up to fifty years.

This has been just a peek at all you could learn with reptile pets. Good luck on all your scaly creature adventures wherever they may lead you!

Puzzle Answers

page 12 • Members Only

Snake, lizard, turtle, tortoise, crocodile, and alligator

page 18 • Code for the Cold

FOLLOW THE PATH TO THE ROTTING LOG. DIG. SLEEP UNTIL SPRING.

page 22 • Terrifying Lizard

ADD, PIN, INK, SON, ASK, PAT, RUN, ARM

The middle letters read: DINOSAUR

Why did the two boa constrictors get married? Because they had a crush on each other!

*Dinosaur means "terrifying lizard."

page 28 • Tasty Treats

RATS

SNAILS

FROG

SNAKE

MOUSE

page 31 • Major Mamba

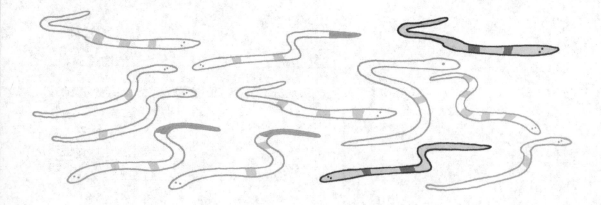

page 33 • Wiggly Way Out

page 37 • Green Garden Gift

What do you give a sick snake? An ASPirin.

page 49 • Get a Gecko!

c. Andy   b. Pedro   d. Colin

page 51 • Komodo Couple

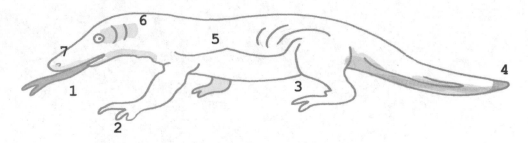

page 53 • Save the Snakes!

Sally's Snake Sanctuary, Pete's Pet Palace, Sarah's Scaly Savers, Gary's Green Gang, Rosie's Reptile Refuge, Larry's Lizard Lounge, Carol's Critter Club, Tina's Tortoise Trailer

page 59 • Tasty Tortoise Tidbits

WEEDS	DANDELION	CALCIUM	CLOVER
CORN	HERBS	WATER	CHICORY
GRASS	CACTUS	FLOWERS	ENDIVE

Tortoises should not eat: DOG OR CAT FOOD

page 62 • Perfect Pot

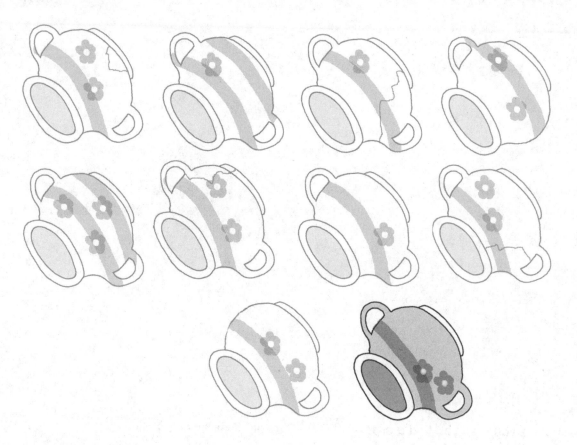

page 66 • Glub Glub!

The green sea turtle spends most of its life in the deep ocean. It can hold its breath under water for five hours at a time while eating seagrass and algae.

page 67 • Turtle Traditions

YERTLE THE TURTLE   TEENAGE MUTANT NINJA TURTLES   KOOPA

page 72 • Crocodile Rockin'

What do you do if you find a crocodile in your toilet? Wait till he's finished!

page 76 • Come On Caiman

I caiman a boat

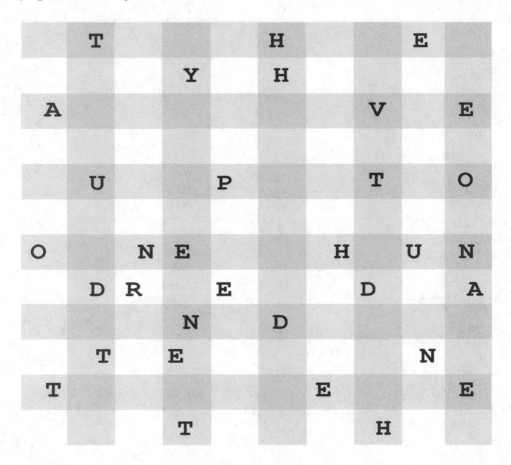

They have up to one hundred and ten teeth.

page 85 • Super Senses

An organ on the lips that is sensitive to heat changes.

page 87 • Turtle Trick

page 92 • Clever Camo

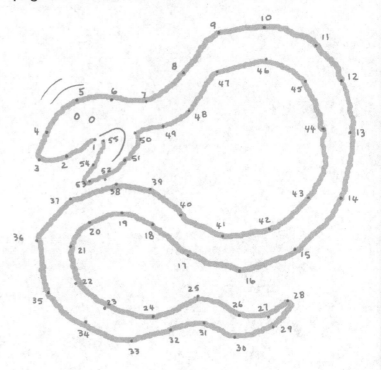

What would you get if you cross a newborn snake with a basketball? A bouncing baby boa!

page 98 • Snake Stories

A hoop snake swallows its tail and rolls after people. False. However, they will often lie in a circle shape when sunning.

Snake jaws are not fused together at the base, allowing them to open to a size much bigger than their heads. True. Snakes have a tube at the base of the mouth that allows them to breathe when their mouth is full.

Snakes can hypnotize their prey with their eyes or body movements. False. What some snakes do is move their head to get a better sense of depth perception—just like we do!

Some snakes have very long fangs that fold back in their mouth when not in use. True. This is so they don't bite themselves.

A milk snake is able to milk a cow. False. Besides not being able to digest milk, they don't have the proper mouth structure to allow them to do this.

Rattlesnakes can't hear anything; they rely on movement and smell. True. Snakes have neither external ears nor moveable eyelids.

page 101 • Hiding in Plain Sight

REPEAT

REPLACE

REPORT

REPLAY

REPAIR

There are 2 two-headed snakes.

What does a snake sign at the bottom of his letters? Love and hisses!

page 113 • Sssnake Ssspeak

This summer I should see how expensive a plane is and go visit South America to see my long lost relatives.

page 115 • Home Sweet Cave

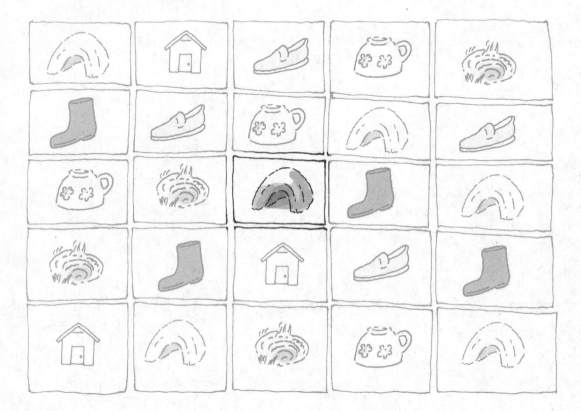

page 125 • Selective Snake

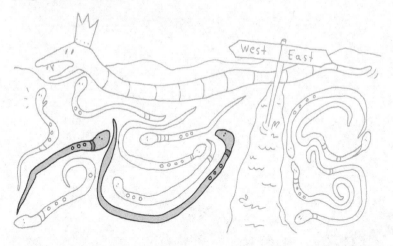

page 127 • Scaredy Skink

page 129 • Tortoise Tricks

Steppe tortoise, Afghanistan tortoise, four-toed tortoise, and Russian box turtle are the real names.